lonely planet

# POCKET
# REYKJAVÍK &
# SOUTHWEST ICELAND

**TOP EXPERIENCES · LOCAL LIFE**

T0018191

**BELINDA DIXON, ALEXIS AVERBUCK,
CAROLYN BAIN, JADE BREMNER**

# Contents

## Plan Your Trip

Harpa (p72)
NIC LEHOUX ©

## Special Features

## COVID-19

We have rechecked every business in this book before publication to ensure that it is still open after the COVID-19 outbreak. However, the economic and social impacts of COVID-19 will continue to be felt long after the outbreak has been contained, and many businesses, services and events referenced in this guide may experience ongoing restrictions. Some businesses may be temporarily closed, have changed their opening hours and services, or require bookings; some unfortunately could have closed permanently. We suggest you check with venues before visiting for the latest information.

# Top Experiences

## See the Icebergs of Jökulsárlón

Icebergs adrift in an ethereal lagoon. **p120**

## Get Wet at the Blue Lagoon

Iceland's luminous landmark lagoon.
**p86**

## Explore the National Museum

Iceland's excellent, comprehensive history museum.
**p34**

# Experience the Wonders of Snæfellsjökull National Park

This national park is a microcosm of Iceland's terrain. **p124**

# Walk through History at Þingvellir National Park

Iceland's stunning rift valley and parliament site. **p96**

## Hallgrímskirkja

Reykjavík's graceful, iconic church.
**p64**

## Feel the Roar at Gullfoss

Gorgeous falls cast rainbow mists.
**p94**

# Go Back in Time at the Settlement Exhibition
Fascinating settler's ruins and multimedia exhibit. **p36**

## The Original Geysir
The original gushing geyser.
**p98**

## Witness the Story of Iceland at the Settlement Centre

Dive deep into Iceland's Saga history. **p134**

## Encountering Whales

Scan chilly waters for majestic whales. **p52**

# Dining Out

*From take-it-to-go hot dogs to gourmet platters on white-clothed tables, little Reykjavík has an astonishing assortment of places to eat. Here, a wealth of Icelandic and 'New Nordic' restaurants serve innovative variations on local fish and lamb. Outside the capital, eateries range from high-end restaurants to simple gas-station grills.*

## Food Culture

Reykjavík has seen a recent surge in restaurant openings, many of the highest standard and expressing all manner of culinary creativity. Cafes by day turn into restaurants and bars at night. Tapas-style dining, high-concept Icelandic cuisine and burger joints all rub shoulders.

## Icelandic Specialities

If you see a queue in Reykjavík, it probably ends at a *pýlsur* (hot dog) stand. *Fiskisúpa*

(fish soup) comes courtesy of family recipes, while *kjötsúpa* (meat soup) usually features veggies and chunks of lamb. Icelandic lamb is hard to beat, with free-range sheep munching chemical-free grasses and herbs. In the past, Icelanders merely kept the cheeks and tongues of *þorskur* (cod) – a delicacy – and exported the rest; but today you'll commonly find cod fillets on the menu, along with *ýsa* (haddock) and *bleikja* (Arctic char). During

the summer, try *silungur* (freshwater trout) and *villtur lax* (wild salmon). Don't miss *skyr*, a yoghurt-like concoction made from pasteurised skimmed milk.

## Top Tips

○ Reserve ahead in summer for top restaurants; service may stop at 9pm.

○ It's not customary to tip.

○ Be aware there are significant conservation issues with whale, puffin and shark.

FROM MY POINT OF VIEW/SHUTTERSTOCK©

## Best Reykjavík Restaurants

**Dill** One of Reykjavík's finest restaurants, with elaborate tasting menus. (p74)

**Matur og Drykkur** Innovative, refined Icelandic cuisine. (p57)

**Þrír Frakkar** Classy, consistently good Icelandic food. (p75)

## Best Seafood Restaurants

**Messinn** Piping hot fish skillets served with aplomb. (p44)

**Fiskfélagið** Fine seafood prepared in seemingly endless ways. (p44)

**Icelandic Fish & Chips** Indulge your fish-fry

fantasy with delicious dips. (p46)

**Hafið Bláa** Super-fresh seafood and divine views right on the South Coast (p117)

## Cheaper Eats

**SKÁL!** Experimental, memorable and super-classy street eats. (p74)

**Hlemmur Mathöll** Gourmet street food in a former bus depot. (p75)

**Grandi Mathöll** Old Harbour food truck eats (p58)

**Flatey Pizza** Reykjavík's best purveyors of sourdough disks (p58)

**Hamborgara Búllan** Legendary burger bar beloved by Hollywood stars. (p59)

## Restaurants Outside Reykjavík

**Efstidalur II** Farm-fresh meals in the Golden Circle. (p103)

**Bjargarsteinn Mathús** Waterfront delights on the Snæfellsnes Peninsula. (p129)

**Gamla Fjósið** South Coast former cowshead delivering marvellously meaty mains. (p115)

**Settlement Centre** Restaurant Icelandic dishes in a heritage-rich room. (p139)

# Bar Open

*Reykjavík's rich coffee culture delivers cool cafes that encourage lingering over morning coffee and light lunches. But as evening comes many undergo a Jekyll-and-Hyde transformation – coffee becomes beer, DJs materialise in dark corners, and suddenly you're in a kick-ass, late-night bar. Beyond the city, towns boast cosy bakeries, while waterfront cafes are a treat in the Snæfellsnes Peninsula and around Borgarnes.*

GPRITCHETTPHOTO/SHUTTERSTOCK©

## Cafe Treats

The old-school Icelandic *bakarí* (bakeries) can't be praised enough. Reykjavík has some superb pastry pit stops, and most towns have at least one.

Icelandic *pönnukökur* (pancakes) are thin, sweet and cinnamon flavoured. Icelandic *kleinur* (twisted doughnuts) are a chewy treat, along with their offspring *ástar pungar* (love balls), deep-fried, spiced balls of dough. You'll find these desserts in bakeries and cafes, along with an amazing array of fantastic pastries and cakes – one of the few sweet legacies of the Danish occupation.

## Hot Dogs & Grills

Icelanders do enjoy fast food – as evidenced by the wealth of hot-dog stands and burger joints. Large petrol stations often have good, cheap, well-patronised grills and cafeterias attached. They generally serve sandwiches and fast food from around 11am to 9pm or 10pm. Some also offer hearty set meals at lunchtime, such as meat soup, fish of the day or plates of lamb.

## Tips for Buying Alcohol

○ You must be at least 20 years old to buy beer, wine or spirits.

○ Most towns have a state-run Vínbúðin liquor store (www.vinbudin.is); opening hours vary wildly.

○ In Reykjavík, early-evening happy hours cut costs to between 700kr and 900kr per beer.

EGILL BJARNASON/LONELY PLANET©

## Best Cafes

**Reykjavík Roasters** The capital's premier coffee aficionados. (p78)

**Kaffi Vínyl** Coffee, cocktails and laid-back tunes. (p76)

**Stofan Kaffihús** Spacious and welcoming in the heart of Old Reykjavík. (p45)

**Kaffi Mokka** A historic cafe with a well-worn feel. (p78)

**Friðheimar** Own-grown grub on a Golden Circle farm. (p107)

**Eldstó Art Café** Icelandic flatbread with smoked lamb. Yum. (p118)

**Black Beach Restaurant** Cool South Cast eatery with fine ocean views (p118)

**Joylato** Reykjavík's favourite ice cream (p76)

**Café Kaffitár** Chilled-out pit stop at Reykjavík's National Museum (p45)

## Best For Craft Beer

**Bryggjan Brugghús** Microbrewery with harbour views. (p61)

**Kaldi** Hipster hangout with house-made brews on tap. (pictured; p69)

**Smiðjan Brugghús** Own-brewed craft ales and tasty burgers in Vík. (p119)

**Skúli Craft Bar** Brews include 14 on tap and 130 in bottles (who's counting?). (p47)

**Steðji Brugghús** Borgarnes microbrewery producing strawberry beer. (p140)

## Best Bakeries

**Bakarí Sandholt** Fresh-baked breads, sandwiches, soups and pastries. (p75)

**Brauð & Co** Excellent handmade loaves, pastries and organic supplies. (p75)

**17 Sortir** Memorable, multi-coloured cupcakes. (p61)

**Nesbrauð** Sweet treats in the Snæfellsnes Peninsula (p130)

# Treasure Hunt

L.LIKA/SHUTTERSTOCK©

*Iceland's, and especially Reykjavík's, vibrant design culture and craft-oriented ethos make for great shopping: from edgy fashion and knitted lopapeysur (Icelandic woollen sweaters) to unique music and lip-smacking liquor. Many artists and designers form collectives and open shops full of handmade work.*

## Sweaters & Knitting

*Lopapeysur* are the ubiquitous Icelandic woolly sweaters you will see worn by locals and visitors alike. Made from naturally water-repellent Icelandic wool, they are thick and cosy, with simple geometric patterns or regional motifs. They are no longer the bargain they were in the 1960s, so when shopping, be sure to make the distinction: do you want hand-knit or machine made?

You'll notice the price difference (some cost well over 27,500kr), but either way these beautiful but practical items (and their associated hats, gloves and scarves) are exceptionally wearable souvenirs.

## Design

Reykjavík's Iceland Design Centre (p49) promotes local designers' work, and you can check online for the latest news, exhibitions and events, as well as interesting blog posts. Its

**DesignMarch** (www. designmarch.is; ⊙Mar) annual event opens hundreds of exhibitions and workshops to the public.

## Best for Music & Books

**12 Tónar** Uber hip record shop; occasional live bands. (p81)

**Lucky Records** Eclectic range of tunes (p81)

**Mál og Menning** Big English-language section - a haven for bookworms. (p80)

**Reykjavík Record Shop** Vinyl all the way. (p81)

ATARICLASH/SHUTTERSTOCK©

## Best for Design

**Akkúrat** The Icelandic Design Centre's concept store (p49)

**Kirsuberjatréð** Top Icelandic arts and crafts in a 19th-century shop. (p49)

**Skúmaskot** Carefully selected crafts from local designers. (p80)

## Best Markets

**Frú Lauga** (p83) Good farmers market in the Laugardalur neighbourhood.

**Kolaportið Flea Market** (p49) Retro rummaging at Reykjavík's weekend market.

## Best for Souvenirs

**Rammagerðin** Loaded with higher-end mementos, art and Icelandic designs. (p80)

**Dogma** T-shirt specialist taking a wry look at the Icelandic tourist trade. (p81)

**Ljómalind** Tempting farmers' market in Borgarnes (p141)

**Gallerí Laugarvatn** Golden Circle crafts (p107)

**Omnom Chocolate** Quality, gorgeously packaged sweet treats (pictured above; p56)

## Best for Fashion

**Kiosk** Couture collective of quality women's clothing. (p80)

**KronKron** Wacky, wonderful Icelandic clothing designs. (p79)

**Kron** Wildly wonderful shoes (p80)

**Handknitting Association of Iceland** Tops for traditional woollen jumpers. (p80)

**Steinunn** Completely creative knits in couture collections. (p61)

# Tours

*A day-long bus tour from Reykjavík is one of the most cost-effective, efficient ways to see spectacular natural wonders if you're on a short holiday. They're also good if you want to combine sightseeing with activities like snowmobiling, horse riding, rafting or scuba diving. Most provide pick up from city accommodation or nearby bus stops.*

## Information

The **tourist office** (Upplýsingamiðstöð Ferðamanna; ☎411 6040; www.visitreykjavik. is; Ráðhús, Tjarnargata 11; ⊙8am-8pm; ☎) has information on guided walking tours, along with loads of free maps and self-guided walking-tour brochures, from *Literary Reykjavík* to *The Neighbourhood of the Gods.*

## Best Reykjavík Tours

### Literary Reykjavík
(www.bokmenntaborgin.is; Tryggvagata 15; admission free; ⊙3pm Thu Jun-Aug)

Crime-fiction themed tours of the centre.

### Free Walking Tour
(www.freewalkingtour.is; admission free; ⊙noon & 2pm Jun-Aug, 1pm Sep-May) Free one-hour Reykjavík tours covering 1.5km.

### TukTuk Tours
(☎788 5500; www.facebook. com/tuktukiceland; Harpa concert hall, Austurbakki 2; from 30min adult/child 4700/2700kr) Zip around town on a tuk tuk.

## Best Adventure Tours

### Icelandic Mountain Guides
(Iceland Rovers; ☎587 9999; www.mountain guides.is; Stórhöfði 33) Respected outfit specialising in mountaineering, trekking and ice climbing.

### Arctic Adventures
(☎562 7000; www. adventures.is) Enthusiastic staff deliver action-filled tours.

### Midgard Adventure
(☎578 3370; www. midgardadventure.is; Dufþaksbraut 14; tours 14,000-34,000kr) One of South Iceland's best adventure operators.

### Inside the Volcano
(☎519 5609; www.inside thevolcano.com; tours 42,000kr; ⊙mid-May–mid-Oct) Go into a 4000-year-old magma chamber.

## Best Horse-Riding Tours

### Eldhestar
(☎480 4800; http://eldhestar.is/tours; Vallavegur, off Hringvegur; 1hr tour adult/child from

BAHADIR YENICERI/SHUTTERSTOCK©

8000/6400kr; ⊙8.45am-4.30pm) Near Hveragerði, rides on surrounding grasslands.

**Íshestar** (📞555 7000; www.ishestar.is; Sörlaskeið 26, Hafnarfjörður; half-/full day 12,200/22,000kr) One of the oldest stables with trots through lava fields.

## Best Air Tours

**Atlantsflug** (📞854 4105; www.flightseeing. is; Reykjavík Domestic Airport; adult/child from 26,900/13,450kr) Offers flightseeing tours from Reykjavík, Bakki Airport and Skaftafell.

**Eagle Air** (📞562 2640; www.eagleair.is; Reykjavík Domestic Airport) Sightseeing flights over volcanoes and glaciers.

**Air Iceland** (📞570 3030; www.airicelandconnect.is; Reykjavík Domestic Airport) Combination air, bus, hiking, rafting, horse-riding, whale-watching and glacier tours.

**Norðurflug** (📞562 2500; www.helicopter. is; Nauthólsvegur 58d, Reykjavík Domestic Airport; Reykjavík flight 27,900kr) Helicopters flights over Reykjavík and beyond.

## Best Bus Tours

**Reykjavík Excursions** (Kynnisferðir; 📞580 5400; www.re.is; BSÍ Bus Terminal, Vatnsmýrarvegur 10; tours 8000-47,300kr) Popular operator; extensive summer and winter programmes.

**Hidden Iceland** (📞770 5733; www.hiddeniceland.is) Enthusiastic off-the-beaten path tours.

**Gateway to Iceland** (📞534 4446; www.gtice. is) Small groups and good guides.

**Go Green** (📞694 9890; www.gogreen.is; tours from 44,000kr) High-end with sustainable practices.

## Best Bicycle Tours

**Reykjavík Bike Tours** (📞694 8956; www.iceland bike.com; Ægisgarður 7; bike rental per 4hr from 3500kr, tours from 7500kr; ⊙9am-5pm Jun-Aug, shorter hours Sep-May; 🚌14) Bike hire and tours of Reykjavík and surrounds.

**Bike Company** (📞590 8550; http://bikecompany. is) Bicycle tours throughout the region.

# Natural Wonders

*It is an absolute must to take a day trip or an overnight outside of Reykjavík to take in some of the incredible volcanic landscapes, geothermal fields, glaciers, dramatic fjords and black-sand seashores. In summer, bird life can be abundant, with puffins flapping and Arctic terns diving. And from October to April look for the Northern Lights.*

## Why Iceland's Rocks Rock

The country sits on the Mid-Atlantic Ridge, a massive 18,000km-long rift between two of the earth's major tectonic plates. Iceland is a shifting, steaming lesson in schoolroom geology. Suddenly you'll be racking your brains to remember long-forgotten homework on how volcanoes work, and why lava and magma aren't quite the same thing.

## What Should We See?

In Iceland's Southwest, it's best to string together the top sights, including the Golden Circle, with more off-the-beaten-path diversions – you'll still even have a bit of time left to lap up Reykjavík's unique charm. Although choosing between incomparable vistas is like trying to pick a favourite child, these lists give you an epic start.

## Best Glaciers

**Vatnajökull** The largest ice cap in Europe with glacier tongues and a giant park. (p112)

**Langjökull** West Iceland's tour-able ice cave. (p137)

**Snæfellsjökull** So awesome it has its own West Iceland national park. (p124)

**Sólheimajökull** Prime place for glacier walks and ice climbs. (p113)

## Best Waterfalls

**Gullfoss** The 'Golden Falls' course over rock tiers and down a gorge. (p94)

**Seljalandsfoss** Walk behind the curtain of this cascade. (p113)

**Skógafoss** Dreamy, 62m-high waterfall. (p112)

MY GOOD IMAGES/SHUTTERSTOCK©

## Best Geothermal Springs

**Blue Lagoon** Vibrant turquoise and worldfamous. (p86)

**Gamla Laugin** Historic Golden Circle spring amid meadows. (p101)

**Krauma** Modern West Iceland spa complex at Europe's biggest hot spring. (p137)

**Sundhöllin** Reykjavík's 1930s swim spot boasts a roof-top pool. (p72)

**Fontana** Chic and lakeside in easy-to-reach Laugarvatn. (p101)

**Lýsuhólslaug** Bubbly water on the south coast of the Snæfellsnes Peninsula. (p131)

**Reykjadalur** Bathe in hot rivers in a geothermal valley. (p102)

## Best Volcanoes

**Hekla** Once thought to be the gates of hell; you can climb it. (p116)

**Eyjafjallajökull** Stopped Europe's air traffic in 2010. (p116)

**Kerið** An multi-hued crater with red earth and a green lake. (p102)

**Eldfell** Small, but almost smothered Heimaey in lava in 1973. (p114)

**Saxhöll** Hike this Snæfellsjökull crater for sweeping lava flow views. (p131)

## Best Lava Tubes

**Viðgelmir** Iceland's largest lava tube is accessible by guided tour. (p137)

**Vatnshellir** Much-loved lava tunnels in Snæfellsjökull National Park. (p128)

## Best Beaches

**Diamond Beach** Where icebergs and black sand meet. (p121)

**Reynisfjara** Basalt columns back this dusky shore. (p112)

**Djúpalón Beach** Rock arches, shipwrecks and black sands. (p127)

**Sandgerði** Bird-rich marshes and shores. (p89)

# Festivals

*Icelanders celebrate festivals with gleeful enthusiasm. While Reykjavík is the epicentre of the excitement, even small villages have their own festivities: for local heroes, civic pride or just good old-fashioned traditions. The Reykjavík festivals are also a super showcase for Icelandic and international music and art.*

ENRIQUE REMBIS/SHUTTERSTOCK©

## Best Music Festivals

**Iceland Airwaves** (www. icelandairwaves.is; ☉Nov) Showcase for new music with around 200 acts from 30 countries.

**Secret Solstice** (www. secretsolstice.is; Engjavegur 7; ☉Jun) Music festival during 24 hours of daylight.

**Þjóðhátíð** (National Festival; www.dalurinn.is; Dalvegur; 23,900kr, ferry price 1380kr; ☉Jul or Aug) 11,000 people descend on Heimaey to listen to bands, watch fireworks, and drink.

**Reykjavík Jazz Festival** (www.reykjavikjazz.is; ☉Aug) Toe-tapping with international acts.

**Innipúkinn Festival** (www.innipukinn.is; ☉Jul) Indie music gatherings held in Reykjavík clubs.

## Best Arts Festival

**Reykjavík Culture Night** (Menningarnótt; www. menningarnott.is; ☉Aug) 24 hours of art, music, dance and fireworks; galleries and churches stay open late.

**Reykjavík International Film Festival** (www.riff. is; ☉Sep) Eleven days of quirky flicks.

**DesignMarch** (www. designmarch.is; ☉Mar) Exhibitions and workshops open to the public.

**Reykjavík Arts Festival** (www.listahatid.is; ☉Jun) Two weeks of theatre, film, dance, music and visual art.

**Reykjavík International Literary Festival** (Bókmenntahátíð; www. bokmenntahatid.is; ☉Apr) Readings and panels with international authors.

## Best Cultural Festivals

**National Day** (☉17 Jun) The country's biggest holiday commemorates the founding of the Republic of Iceland in 1944 with parades and patriotic merriness.

**Reykjavík Pride** (www. hinsegindagar.is; ☉Aug) Some 100,000 people celebrate LGBTIQ+ culture and traditions.

**Þorrablót** A Viking midwinter feast marked with stomach-churning treats.

**Beer Day** (☉1 Mar) The whole country celebrates the day, in 1989, when the prohibition on beer was overturned. It gets lively...

**Food & Fun** (www. foodandfun.is; ☉Mar) International chefs join local restaurants to compete for awards.

# Museums & Galleries

*In terms of first-rate galleries and museums, small-city Reykjavík punches well above its weight. The capital's contemporary art, photography and sculpture collections in particular truly shine. Heritage and cultural displays are creatively curated too - with museums in Reykjavík and the Southwest covering everything from Settlement and the sagas, to the Northern Lights.*

REYKJAVÍK ART MUSEUM–HAFNARHÚS.
PHOTO: HILDUR INGA BJÖRNSDÓTTIR©

## Best Art Museums & Galleries

**Reykjavík Art Museum** Three superb branches on one ticket. (pictured; p41)

**National Gallery of Iceland** Constantly changing collection of Iceland's finest works. (p72)

**Kling & Bang** Features cutting-edge young artists. (p57)

**Sigurjón Ólafsson Museum** Oceanside sculpture with sea breezes, totem poles and busts. (p83)

**Reykjavík Museum of Photography** Superbly curated collection of images (p43)

## Best History Museums

**National Museum** All of Iceland's best artefacts gathered under one well curated roof. (p34)

**Culture House** Brilliantly evokes Iceland's past, from settlement to today. (p72)

**Settlement Exhibition** Excellent multimedia exhibits and an excavated Viking longhouse. (p36)

**Reykjavík Maritime Museum** Powerful stories from the fishing industry. (p56)

**Settlement Centre** Sagas and the birth of Iceland in compelling displays (p134)

**Norska Húsið** Old wooden Snæfellsnes house packed with characterful antiques. (p127)

**Volcano Museum** Art, artefacts and lava chunks. (p129)

## Best Off-Beat Exhibitions

**Icelandic Phallological Museum** Fascinating, array of Icelandic penises. (p73)

**Draugasetrið** Goulish haunted house in Stokkseyri (p115)

# For Free

*Although alive with cosmopolitan bustle, Reykjavík is a city that begs to be explored, for free, on foot. Stroll from your priceless photo op at towering Hallgrímskirkja, via the characterful old town to the free galleries of the revitalised Grandi area. Further afield, Iceland's blockbuster wild spaces also come without an entrance fee.*

GILBERTGOON/SHUTTERSTOCK©

## Best Natural Wonders

**Geysir** Watch the geothermal water spout like clockwork. (p98)

**Gullfoss** The famous Golden Falls tumble down a narrow canyon. (p94)

**Reynisfjara** Black-sand beach near Vík with basalt columns, caves and sea stacks (p112)

**Breiðafjörður** Broad islet-dotted waterway off the Snæfellsnes Peninsula (p128)

**Dyrhólaey** Prime puffin-watching on the South Coast. (p112)

**Eldfell** Get climbing a 221-m high volcano. (p114)

## Best Art & Architecture

**Hallgrímskirkja** Wander the church grounds and look inside, though the tower will cost ya. (pictured; p64)

**Marshal House** Three cutting-edge art spaces under one roof. (p57)

**i8** Superb modern Icelandic art (p43)

**Sun Voyager** Skeletal, shiplike sculpture beloved by photographers. (p73)

**Harpa** The city's shimmering, cavernous concert hall. (p72)

**Einar Jónsson Sculpture Garden** Brilliant collections of bronzes. (p67)

**Viðey Island** Art installations including Yoko Ono's *Imagine Peace Tower.* (p84)

## Best Local

**Old Harbour** Along with neighbouring Grandi, it's a prime people watching spot. (p51)

**Reykjavík Botanic Gardens** Home to over 5000 varieties of subarctic plants. (p83)

**Laugardalur** A green Reykjavík parkland jammed with activity options. (p82)

**Borg á Mýrum** Atmospheric Borgarnes farm with strong saga links. (p135)

**Tjörnin** Reykjavík's 'Pond' echoes with the honks and squawks of more than 40 bird species. (p41)

**Skógar Folk Museum** People-centred insights into local life (p114)

**Alþingi** Free visits to the Icelandic parliament. (p43)

# Under the Radar Reykjavík

*Iceland has a strong alternative music history. It has spawned international names like Björk, The Sugarcubes, Hafdis Huld and Emiliana Torrini, Sigur Rós and Of Monsters and Men. Reykjavík's live scene is uber-creative, welcoming, and a chance to rub shoulders with the locals while experiencing diverse, experimental Nordic sounds.*

CHALIE CHULAPORNSIRI/SHUTTERSTOCK©

## Best Off-Beat Exhibitions

**Icelandic Phallological Museum** Fascinating, array of Icelandic penises. (pictured; p73)

**Draugasetrið** Goulish haunted house in Stokkseyri (p115)

## Best Bar Venues

**Hurrá** Hipsters like this joint, showing a vast range of live music nearly every night. (p48)

**Dillon** Beer, beards and a tiny corner stage hosting rock bands. (p69)

**Gaukurinn** Every night is different, it could be drag night or heavy metal at this grungy place. (p48)

**Prikið** Hosts most live music, and has a reputation for hip hop, grime and rap. (p69)

**KEX Bar** Jazz, bebop, swing and boogie-woogie and everything in between. (p77)

## Best Small Venues

**Mengi** Intimate arty space showcasing experimental musicians has a record store on site. (p79)

**Iðnó Theatre** A handsome theatre dating back to 1897, with a range of live performances. (p49)

**Hannesarholt** Home to Iceland's former prime minister, Hannes Hafstein, in 1915, this is one of the most esteemed concerned venues. The place to catch opera or classic piano music. (p79)

**Lucky Records** Acts are frequently hosted at this record store crammed with vinyl. (p81)

**Nordic House** The place for Norwegian Jazz to Nordic Folk Music. (p48)

## Best Clubs

**Paloma** A tight basement room where DJs spin reggae, electronica and pop (p46)

**Pablo Discobar** Neon-bright, nostalgic, DJ playing cheesy pop, always a good time. (p46)

# For Kids

*Reykjavík, and Iceland, are supremely child-friendly places, thanks to a tempting variety of attractions and facilities. Most kids find the whole country an adventure with its wide-open spaces, wildlife and science projects brought to life. Prepare for bird colonies, waterfalls and volcanic areas; child-friendly activities include short hikes, super-Jeep tours, horse riding, whale watching and boat rides.*

NEJA HROVAT/SHUTTERSTOCK©

## Best Day Trips

**Viðey Island** Bike and hike on a windswept coastal island. (pictured; p84)

**Geysir** Watch the geyser shoot water wonderfully high. (p98)

**River Rafting** Strap 'em in for a zip down the Hvítá river. (p104)

## Best Parks

**Reykjavík Zoo & Family Park** What's not to love? Farm animals, floaty rafts and kids' rides. (p83)

**Tjörnin** Get your crumbs and feed the ducks at the pretty lake. (p41)

**Hljómskálagarður** Examine interesting sculptures throughout the park. (p39)

**Geothermal Park** Boil an egg in the thermal vents in Hveragerði. (p101)

**Icelandic Goat Centre** Cute bovidae with surprising *Game of Thrones* links. (p139)

## Best Sights

**Hallgrímskirkja** Take the elevator to the top of the church for thrilling views. (p64)

**Volcano House** Watch movies of eruptions. (p43)

**Saga Museum** See silicon representations of the Sagas, then dress up in costume for photos. (p56)

**Whales of Iceland** Look at amazing life-size replicas of all the Icelandic whales. (p56)

**Omnom Chocolate** Tour a local chocolate factory. (p56)

**Aurora Reykjavík** Try out the Northern Lights simulator. (p56)

**Kerið** Peer into a 6500-year old volcano crater (p102)

## Best Swims

**Laugardalslaug** Giant outdoor geothermal pool complex with water slide. (p83)

**Blue Lagoon** Teal water and silica mud for horseplay. (p86)

**Gamla Laugin** Huge geothermal pool by a burbling stream. (p101)

# LGBTIQ+

*Iceland is not only tolerant of, but is also proud of, its LGBTIQ+ traditions. This is after all the country where an enthusiasm for Gay Pride sees rainbow flags lining the streets, and a LGBTIQ+-friendly vibe holds sway. But you won't find swaths of gay bars here – it's more that low-key, almost casual acceptance rules.*

SERGEY DIDENKO/SHUTTERSTOCK©

In Iceland a broad sense of LGTBIQ+ acceptance has transferred to the ballot box: in 2009 the world's first openly gay prime minister, Jóhanna Sigurðardóttir, came to power here.

In general, Icelanders have a very open, accepting attitude towards the LGBTIQ+ community, though the scene remains fairly subtle.

## Best Gay Iceland

**Reykjavík Pride** (www. hinsegindagar.is; ⏰Aug) A fantastical festival bringing carnival-like colour to the capital to celebrate LGBTIQ+ culture and traditions. Some 100,000 people (the equivalent of more than 25% of the country's population) attend the Pride march and celebrations.

**Kiki** (www.kiki.is; Laugavegur 22; ⏰8pm-1am Wed, Thu & Sun, to 4.30am Fri & Sat) Ostensibly a queer bar, Kiki is also the place to get your dance on, with pop and electronica the mainstays.

**Pink Iceland** (☎562 1919; www.pinkiceland.is; Hverfisgata 39; ⏰9am-5pm Mon-Fri) Iceland's first gay-and-lesbian owned-and-focused travel agency welcomes all. It arranges all manner of travel, events and weddings and offers tours, including a two-hour happy-hour walking tour of Reykjavík (6000kr).

**Samtökin '78** (☎552 7878; www.samtokin78. is; Suðurgata 3; ⏰office 1-4pm Mon-Fri, Queer Centre 8-11pm Thu, closed Jul) The gay organisation provides information during office hours and operates a community centre on Thursday nights.

**Visit Gayice** (www.gayice. is) and **Gay Iceland** (www. gayiceland.is) for LGBTIQ+ tips and news.

**Literary Reykjavík** (www.bokmenntaborgin.is; Tryggvagata 15; admission free; ⏰3pm Thu Jun-Aug) Has a Culture Walks app with a Queer Literature feature.

# Four Perfect Days

## Day 1

RÁÐHÚS, REYKJAVÍK ©

Explore historic Old Reykjavík – the **Ráðhús** (pictured above; p43) and the city's best museums, such as the impressive **National Museum** (p34) or evocative **Settlement Exhibition** (p36).

Eat at hip **Nora Magasin** (p46), then wander up arty Skólavörðustígur, browsing jewellery at **Orrifinn** (p81) and photographing the immense **Hallgrímskirkja** (p64). Nearby sits shopping drag Laugavegur, and the **Kiosk** (p80), **Kron** (p80) and **KronKron** (p79) boutiques.

Dine at lively **Hlemmur Mathöll** (p75) before craft beer at **Mikkeller & Friends** (p76), joining Reykjavík's *djammið* pub crawl, and a late-night dance at **Kiki** (p69).

## Day 2

TAKEPICSFORFUN/SHUTTERSTOCK ©

Get a fix of Old Harbour sea air on a **whale-watching tour** (pictured above; p53) or waterfront stroll. Next comes brunch at **Kaffivagninn** (p59), tours of the revamped **Reykjavík Maritime Museum** (p56), and the fabulous, free **Kling & Bang** (p57) art space. Refuel on top-notch fish at **Bergsson RE** (p59) or gourmet pizzas at **Flatey** (p58).

Visit Laugardalur, east of the city centre, to be immersed in **geothermal pools** (p83) and cool art at the **Sigurjón Ólafsson Museum** (p83).

Book ahead to dine at **Dill** (p74), then opt for cocktails at **Pablo Discobar** (p47), a show at **Harpa** (p72), movie at **Bíó Paradís** (p79) or live music at **Mengi** (p79).

## Day 3

Time to hit the road; rent your own wheels or join a day tour.

Explore the rift and historic parliament site at **Þingvellir** (p96), then lunch in Laugarvatn on local fare at **Lindin** (p103).

After spouting **Geysir** (p98) and cascading **Gullfoss** (pictured above; p94), **raft rivers** (p104) out of Reykholt or soak at the **Gamla Laugin** (p101) springs. If you're tired, head home, stopping for dinner at **Tryggvaskáli** (p104) in Selfoss or **Varma** (p104) in Hveragerði.

If you're not visiting the **Blue Lagoon** (p86) on your way to or from the airport, go late this evening, after the crowds have dwindled, before returning to Reykjavík. Fancy a late-night snack? It's got to be **Bæjarins Beztu** (p46).

## Day 4

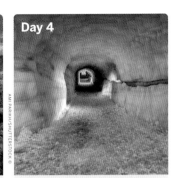

Choose between the wonderful west or the scenic south. If west wins, start at Borgarnes' **Settlement Centre** (p134); if you're heading south, drive to Hella for **horse riding** (p119), visit the falls at **Seljalandsfoss** (p113) or take a guided glacier walk on **Sólheimajökull** (p113).

In the west, explore lava tubes at **Viðgelmir** (p137), the **Langjökull Ice Cave** (pictured above; p137), or go whale watching from **Snæfellsjökull** (p124). In the south, be wowed by **Reynisfjara** (p112) beach and the **Dyrhólaey** (p112) rock arch. End with dinner in Grundarfjörður at **Bjargarsteinn Mathús** (p129).

In the south, take in Vatna-jökull's **glacier tongues** (p112) and **Jökulsárlón** (p120) glacier lagoon.

# Need to Know

For detailed information, see Survival Guide p143.

**Currency**
Icelandic króna (kr)

**Language**
Icelandic; English widely spoken.

**Visas**
Generally not required for stays of up to 90 days. Iceland is a member of the Schengen Convention.

**Money**
Credit cards reign supreme, even in rural areas (PIN required for some purchases, such as petrol). ATMs available in all towns.

**Mobile Phones**
Widespread coverage. Visitors with GSM phones can make roaming calls.

**Time**
Western European Time Zone (GMT/UTC), but there's no daylight saving time.

**Tipping**
Not customary.

## Daily Budget

**Budget: Less than 25,000kr**
Camping: 1500–1800kr
Dorm bed: 5000–7000kr
Grill-bar grub or soup lunch: 1600–2300kr
10,700kr

**Midrange: 25,000–41,000kr**
Guesthouse double room: 19,500–28,000kr
Cafe meal: 1900–4500kr
Museum entry: 1000kr
Pool entry: 650–950kr
Small-vehicle rental per day: 8000kr

**Top End: More than 41,000kr**
Boutique double room: 31,000–51,500kr
Main dish in top restaurant: 3500–7000kr
Spa day pass: 5800kr
4WD rental per day: from 15,000kr

## Advance Planning

**Three to six months before** Book all accommodation; demand always outstrips supply.

**One month before** Book adventure and bus tours.

**One week before** Reserve tables at top restaurants. Pre-book the airport bus, and Blue Lagoon tickets if you want to hit the lagoon on arrival.

# Arriving in Reykjavík

Iceland's primary international airport, Keflavík International Airport, is 48km west of Reykjavík, on the Reykjanes Peninsula. It has money exchange, ATMs, car rental, duty-free shops, cafes and mini-marts.

## ✈ From Keflavík International Airport

**Bus** Flybus, Airport Express and Airport Direct run buses linking the airport with Reykjavík (from 2700kr one way; 50 minutes). They all offer accommodation pick up. Strætó bus 55 connects the BSÍ Bus Terminal and the airport (1840kr, nine daily Monday to Friday in summer).

**Taxis** Cost around 16,100kr to the the centre of Reykjavík.

# Getting Around

## 🚗 Car

A car is unnecessary in compact Reykjavík, but car and camper hire are good for wider excursions. Hire points include airports and the BSÍ Bus Terminal. City speed limits are usually 50km/h (30mph) unless posted otherwise. Seatbelts are required.It is illegal to drive and use a mobile phone.

## 🚌 Local Buses

Strætó runs Reykjavík's buses and has online schedules and a smartphone app. Many free maps also include bus routes. Fares (460kr) can be paid on board or via the app.

## 🚌 Regional Buses

Iceland has a decent bus network running from around mid-May to mid-September between major destinations. Outside this time, services are less frequent (or nonexistent).

Reykjavík

# Reykjavík Neighbourhoods

**Viðey**

**Laugardalur**

**Old Harbour (p51)**
This pretty district boasts some prime arts attractions, a compelling museum, and a great eating and drinking scene.

**Laugavegur & Skólavörðustígur (p63)**
Laugavegur is Reykjavík's premier shopping street and centre for cool cafes, bars and restaurants. Its arty cousin Skólavörðustígur leads to famous Hallgrímskirkja.

**Whale Watching**

**Settlement Exhibition**

**Hallgrímskirkja**

**National Museum**

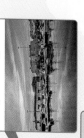

**Old Reykjavík (p33)**
Reykjavík's ancient heart lies here, with its remains of a Viking longhouse, interesting architecture and top museums.

# Explore Reykjavík

*Reykjavík is strikingly cosmopolitan for its size, and loaded with captivating art, rich culinary choices and cool cafes and bars. Add a backdrop of snow-topped mountains, churning seas and crystal-clear air, and the chances are you'll fall helplessly in love.*

# Explore ◈
# Old Reykjavík

*Old Reykjavík is the jaunty heart of the capital. Anchored by the placid Tjörnin lake, the neighbourhood is loaded with brightly coloured houses and absorbing sights. Old Reykjavík is also tops for a wander: from the seafront to Austurvöllur park, via the Alþingi (Parliament) and on to the National Museum.*

*Start exploring historic Reykjavík with a stroll beside Tjörnin (p41), pausing to admire the Ráðhús (p43) and tour the artefact-laden National Museum (p34) en route. The museum's Café Kaffitár (p45) dishes up wholesome food for lunch. Next be absorbed by the Viking longhouse and high-tech displays at the Settlement Exhibition (p36). Mark happy hour at Skúli Craft Bar (p47) and sample acclaimed fish dishes at Fiskmarkaðurinn (p44) or tapas-style dining at Apotek (p44). After, there's still time to sip pints at Micro Bar (p47), quaff cocktails at Loftið (p46) or catch filmic eruptions at the Volcano House (p43); it stays open until 10pm.*

## Getting There & Around

🏃 Old Reykjavík is super compact and walkable. You'll get to most places on foot.

🚌 City buses 1, 3, 6, 11, 12, 13 and 14 from Hlemmur all stop in Old Reykjavík at Lækjartorg and Ráðhús. Bus 14 connects Laugardalur, Hlemmur and Old Reykjavík, and the Old Harbour.

## Old Reykjavík Map on p40

Alþingi (p43) on the shores of Tjörnin (p41)
DENNIS VAN DE WATER/SHUTTERSTOCK ©

Top Experience 📷

# Explore the National Museum

*The superb National Museum beautifully displays Icelandic artefacts from settlement to the modern age, providing a meaningful overview of Iceland's history and culture. Brilliantly curated exhibits lead you through the struggle to settle and organise the forbidding island, the radical changes wrought by the introduction of Christianity, the lean times of domination by foreign powers and Iceland's eventual independence.*

◉ MAP P40, A6

Þjóðminjasafn Íslands

📲 530 2200

www.nationalmuseum.is

Suðurgata 41

adult/child 2000kr/free

🕙 10am-5pm May–mid-Sep, closed Mon mid-Sep–Apr

🚌 1, 3, 6, 12, 14

## Settlement-Era Finds

The premier section of the museum describes the Settlement Era, and features swords, meticulously carved drinking horns, and silver hoards. A powerful bronze figure of Thor is thought to date from about 1000.

## Domestic Life

Exhibits explain how the chieftains ruled and how people survived on little, lighting their dark homes and fashioning bog iron. There's everything from the remains of early *skyr* (Icelandic yoghurt) production to intricate pendants and brooches. Look for the Viking-era *hnefatafl* game set (a bit like chess); this artefact's discovery in a grave in Baldursheimar led to the founding of the museum.

## Viking Graves

Encased in the floor, you'll find Viking-era graves, with their precious burial goods: horse bones, a sword, pins, a ladle and a comb. One of the tombs containing an eight-month-old infant is the only one of its kind ever found.

## Ecclesiastical Artefacts

The section of the museum that details the introduction of Christianity is chock-a-block with rare art and artefacts. For example, the priceless 13th-century Valþjófsstaðir church door.

## The Modern Era

Upstairs, collections span from 1600 to today and give a clear sense of how Iceland struggled under foreign rule, finally gained independence and went on to modernise. Look for the papers and belongings of Jón Sigurðsson, the architect of Iceland's independence.

★ **Top Tips**

o The free smartphone audio guide adds loads of useful detail. The one for kids is in Icelandic or English only.

o Leave a little extra time for the museum's rotating photographic exhibitions.

o Free English tours run at 11am on Wednesday, Saturday and Sunday.

✕ **Take a Break**

The ground-floor Café Kaffitár (p45) offers wi-fi and a welcome respite, with wraparound windows looking out on a flowing fountain.

**Anddyri**

Anddyri með steinlögðu gólfi var byggt við skálann.

**Veggir**

Veggirnir voru að mestu leyti úr torfi af þeirri gerð sem kallast "strengur".

**Básar**

Básar húsdýra voru undir sama þaki og híbýli manna.

**Anteroom**

An anteroom with a partially paved floor was added to the longhouse.

**Walls**

The Walls were made of long, thin strips of turf, called "strengur".

**Animal stalls**

The Animal stalls occupied the same building as the living quarters.

Top Experience 📷

# Go Back in Time at the Settlement Exhibition

*This fascinating museum is based around a 10th-century Viking longhouse and other Settlement Era finds from central Reykjavík. Fine exhibitions imaginatively combine technological wizardry and archaeology to give a glimpse into early Icelandic life. The excavations in Reykjavík have left the site's curators and archaeo-anthropologists with a passion for bringing history to life.*

◎ MAP P40, B3

Landnámssýningin

📞 411 6370

www.reykjavikmuseum.is

Aðalstræti 16

adult/child 1650kr/free

🕘 9am-6pm

## Viking Longhouse

The entire museum is constructed around a 10th-century Viking longhouse unearthed here on Aðalstræti between 2001 and 2002. Mainly a series of foundation walls now, it was thought to be inhabited for only 60 years. Exhibits to look out for are areas with animal bones deliberately built into the structure (for good fortune, perhaps), and the old spring.

## Boundary Wall

Tephra layers are the layer of fragments from a volcanic eruption, and are used to date sites around Iceland. The longhouse was built on top of the 871 layer, but don't miss the fragment of boundary wall at the back of the museum, which was found *below* the tephra layer, and is thus older still. It's the oldest human-made structure in Reykjavík.

## Ancient Artefacts

Arcing around the side of the exhibit, softly lit niches contain artefacts found in the area, ranging from great auk bones (the bird is now extinct) to fish-oil lamps and an iron axe. Recent finds from ancient workshops near the current Alþingi include a silver bracelet and a spindle whorl (for making thread) inscribed with runes (reading 'Vilborg owns me').

## High-Tech Displays

Among the captivating high-tech displays are interactive multimedia tables explaining the area's excavations, which span several city blocks; a wraparound panorama showing how things would have looked at the time of the longhouse; and a space-age-feeling panel that allows you to steer through different layers of the longhouse's construction.

★ **Top Tips**

o Excellent English-language tours run at 11am on weekdays from June to August.

o Multilingual audio guides are free.

o The museum's fun kids' corner has traditional Icelandic toys, rune spelling exercises and computer games.

✗ **Take a Break**

Stroll up to the area just north of Tjörnin to wholesome **Bergsson Mathús** (Map p40, C3; 📞571 1822; www.bergs son.is; Templarasund 3; mains 2200-2800kr; ⏰7am-7pm Mon-Fri, to 5pm Sat & Sun; 🖉) for a casual lunch or brunch, popular with locals.

Or head to the Austurvöllur Sq area, where cafes and bars such as **Café Paris** (Map p40, D2; 📞551 1020; www.cafeparis. is; Austurstræti 14; mains 3000-5600kr; ⏰8.30am-10pm Sun-Thu, to 11pm Fri & Sat; 🛜) spill onto the park in warmer months.

# Walking Tour 🥾

## Historic Reykjavík

*The earliest signs of settlement in Reykjavík date to just before 871 and are centred in the Old Reykjavík quarter. Norwegian Viking Ingólfur Arnarson is credited with being the country's first permanent inhabitant. He made his home in a promising-looking bay that he named Reykjavík (Smoky Bay), after the steam from its thermal springs. This walk takes in the highlights of Ingólfur's historic neighbourhood.*

**Start** Aðalstræti 10
**End** National Museum
**Length** 1.6km; 1½ hours

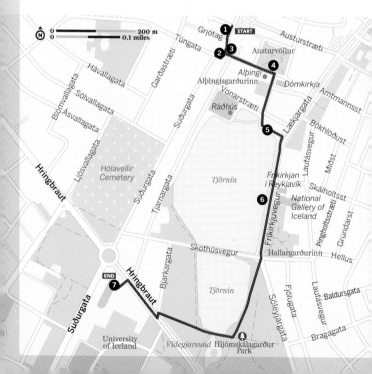

# ❶ Historic House

Reykjavík's oldest timber house dates to 1762, and sits on Aðalstræti, one of the capital's oldest streets. The house is now home to **Aðalstræti 10** (admission free; ◷9am-4pm), which contains changing exhibits about the city's history.

# ❷ Settlement Exhibition

Beneath the Settlement Exhibition (p36) lies a 10th-century Viking longhouse. Curators have augmented the building's dimly lit mood with intriguing multimedia displays.

# ❸ Skúli Magnússon Statue

Across from the Settlement Exhibition, there's a statue of powerful town magistrate-sheriff Skúli Magnússon (1711–94), who organised the building of weaving, tanning and wool-dyeing factories in the capital –the foundations of the modern city of Reykjavík.

# ❹ Austurvöllur

Grassy Austurvöllur park sits next to the Alþingi (parliament; p43) and in its centre there's a statue of Jón Sigurðsson (1811–79), who led the campaign for Icelandic independence. The city's cathedral, Dómkirkja (p43), sits next door.

## ✖ Take a Break

Stop for a coffee on Austurvöllur square, or across the street at smart bistro Nora Magasin (p46) for a quick tipple or a more substantial meal.

# ❺ Iðnó

As you approach lake Tjörnin, you'll see the waterside Ráðhús (city hall; p43). Iðnó (Iðnaðarmannahúsið; The Craftsmen's House) was designed and built by Einar Pálsson in 1896 and was the city's main meeting hall, and for many years a theatre.

# ❻ Around Tjörnin

As you make your way around the banks of Tjörnin (p41), which is called 'the Pond' by locals, you'll pass the quaint church, **Fríkirkjan í Reykjavík**, the National Gallery of Iceland (p72) and **Hljómskálagarður Park** (admission free), which contains sculptures by five historic Icelandic artists.

# ❼ National Museum

The National Museum (p34) traces human history in Iceland, from the earliest settlement to the modern era. There are also rotating photographic exhibits and a welcoming cafe.

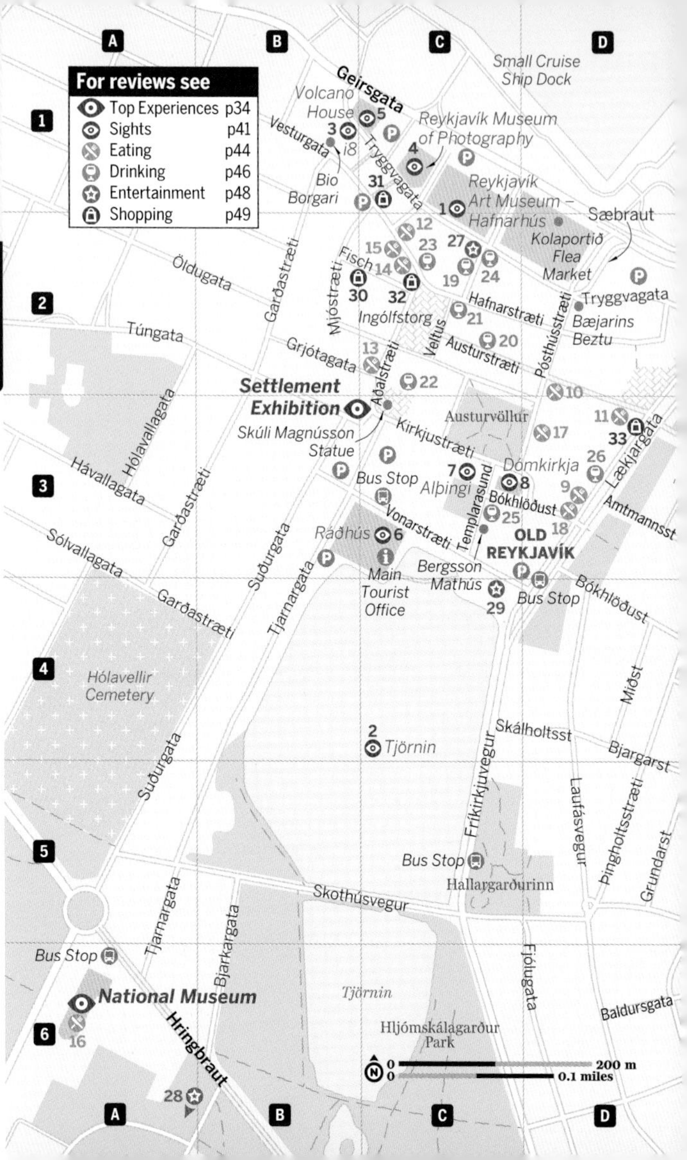

For reviews see
Top Experiences p34
Sights p41
Eating p44
Drinking p46
Entertainment p48
Shopping p49
A
B
C
D
1
2
3
4
5
6
Small Cruise Ship Dock
Geirsgata
Volcano House
Reykjavík Museum of Photography
Vesturgata
i8
Tryggvagata
Bio Borgari
Reykjavík Art Museum – Hafnarhús
Sæbraut
Kolaportið Flea Market
Öldugata
Garðastræti
Mjóstræti
Fischersund
Ingólfstorg
Veltus
Hafnarstræti
Pósthússtræti
Tryggvagata
Bæjarins Beztu
Túngata
Grjótagata
Aðalstræti
Austurstræti
Settlement Exhibition
Skúli Magnússon Statue
Austurvöllur
Kirkjustræti
Hólavallagata
Hávallagata
Garðastræti
Bus Stop
Alþingi
Templarasund
Dómkirkja
Bókhlöðust
Lækjargata
Amtmannsst
Vonarstræti
OLD REYKJAVÍK
Ráðhús
Main Tourist Office
Bergsson Mathús
Bus Stop
Bókhlöðust
Sólvallagata
Suðurgata
Tjarnargata
Garðastræti
Hólavellir Cemetery
Miðst
Skálholtsst
Tjörnin
Bjargarst
Suðurgata
Fríkirkjuvegur
Laufásvegur
Pingholtsstræti
Grundarst
Bus Stop
Hallargarðurinn
Skothúsvegur
Tjarnargata
Bjarkargata
Bus Stop
National Museum
Hringbraut
Tjörnin
Hljómskálagarður Park
Fjólugata
Baldursgata
0 200 m
0 0.1 miles
1
2
3
4
5
6
7
8
9
10
11
12
13
14
15
16
17
18
19
20
21
22
23
24
25
26
27
28
29
30
31
32
33

# Sights

### Reykjavík Art Museum – Hafnarhús    GALLERY

1 ⊙ MAP P40, C1

Reykjavík Art Museum's Hafnarhús is a marvellously restored warehouse converted into a soaring steel-and-concrete exhibition space. Though the well-curated exhibitions of cutting-edge contemporary Icelandic art change frequently (expect installations, videos, paintings and sculpture), you can always count on the comic-book-style paintings of Erró (Guðmundur Guðmundsson), a political artist who has donated several thousand works to the museum. (✎ 411 6400; www.artmuseum.is; Tryggvagata 17; adult/child 1650kr/free; ⊙ 10am-5pm Fri-Wed, to 10pm Thu; 🚌 1, 3, 6, 11, 12, 13, 14)

### Tjörnin    LAKE

2 ⊙ MAP P40, C4

The placid lake at the centre of the city is sometimes locally called the Pond. It echoes with the honks and squawks of more than 40 species of visiting birds, including swans, geese and Arctic terns; feeding the ducks is a popular pastime for the under-fives. Pretty sculpture-dotted parks such as Hljómskálagarður line the southern shores, and their paths are much used by cyclists and joggers. In winter hardy souls strap on ice skates and the lake transforms into an outdoor rink.

Tjörnin

# Icelandic
# Settlement & Sagas

Rumour, myth and fantastic tales of fierce storms and barbaric dog-headed people kept most explorers away from the great northern ocean, *oceanus innavigabilis*. Irish monks who regularly sailed to the Faroe Islands looking for seclusion were probably the first to stumble upon Iceland. It's thought that they settled around the year 700 but fled when Norsemen began to arrive in the early 9th century.

## The Age of Settlement

The Age of Settlement is traditionally defined as between 870 and 930, when political strife on the Scandinavian mainland caused many to flee. Most North Atlantic Norse settlers were ordinary citizens: farmers and merchants who settled across Western Europe, marrying Britons, Westmen (Irish) and Scots.

Among Iceland's first Norse visitors was Norwegian Flóki Vilgerðarson, who uprooted his farm and headed for Snæland around 860. He navigated with ravens, which, after some trial and error, led him to his destination and provided his nickname, Hrafna-Flóki (Raven-Flóki). Hrafna-Flóki sailed to Vatnsfjörður on the west coast but became disenchanted with the conditions. On seeing the icebergs in the fjord he dubbed the country Ísland (Iceland) and returned to Norway. He did eventually settle in Iceland's Skagafjörður district.

According to the 12th-century *Íslendingabók* (a historical narrative of the Settlement Era), Ingólfur Arnarson fled Norway with his blood brother Hjörleifur, landing at Ingólfshöfði (southeast Iceland) in 871. They continued around the coast, and Ingólfur was then led to Reykjavík by a pagan ritual: he tossed his high-seat pillars (a symbol of authority) into the sea as they approached land. Wherever the gods brought the pillars ashore would be the new home of the settlers. Ingólfur named Reykjavík (Smoky Bay) after the steam from its thermal springs. Hjörleifur settled near the present town of Vík, but was murdered by his slaves shortly thereafter.

## The Saga Age

The late 12th century kicked off the Saga Age, when the epic tales of the earlier 9th- to 10th-century settlement were recorded by historians and writers. These sweeping prose epics, or 'sagas', detail the family struggles, romance, vendettas and colourful characters of Settlement, and are the backbone of medieval Icelandic literature, and a rich source for historical understanding.

## i8
GALLERY

3 ⊙ MAP P40, B1

Displays works by some of the country's top modern artists, many of whom show overseas as well. (☎551 3666; www.i8.is; Tryggvagata 16; admission free; ⊙11am-6pm Tue-Fri, 1-5pm Sat)

## Reykjavík Museum of Photography
MUSEUM

4 ⊙ MAP P40, C1

This gallery room, high above Reykjavík City Library, is well worth a visit for its top-notch exhibitions of regional photographers. If you take the lift up, descend by the stairs, which are lined with vintage B&W photos. (Ljósmyndasafn Reykjavíkur; ☎411 6390; www.photomuseum.is; 6th fl, Tryggvagata 15, Grófarhús; adult/child 1000kr/free; ⊙10am-6pm Mon-Thu, 11am-6pm Fri, 1-5pm Sat & Sun)

## Volcano House
MUSEUM

5 ⊙ MAP P40, C1

This modern theatre with a hands-on lava exhibit in the foyer screens a 55-minute pair of films (hourly) about the Vestmannaeyjar volcanoes and Eyjafjallajökull. They show in German, French, Icelandic or Swedish once daily during the summer. (☎555 1900; www.volcanohouse.is; Tryggvagata 11; adult/child 1990/1000kr; ⊙9am-10pm)

## Ráðhús
NOTABLE BUILDING

6 ⊙ MAP P40, C3

Reykjavík's waterside Ráðhús is a beautifully positioned postmodern construction of concrete stilts, tinted windows and mossy walls rising from Tjörnin. Inside you'll find an interesting 3D topographical map of Iceland and the main tourist office (p150). (City Hall; Vonarstræti; admission free; ⊙8am-4pm Mon-Fri)

## Alþingi
HISTORIC BUILDING

7 ⊙ MAP P40, C3

Iceland's first parliament, the Alþingi, was created at Þingvellir in AD 930. After losing independence in the 13th century, the country gradually won back its autonomy, and the modern Alþingi moved into this current basalt building in 1881. A stylish glass-and-stone annexe was completed in 2002. Visitors can attend sessions (four times weekly mid-September to early June) when parliament is sitting; see the website for details. (☎563 0500; www.althingi.is; Kirkjustræti; admission free)

## Dómkirkja
CHURCH

8 ⊙ MAP P40, C3

Iceland's main cathedral, 18th-century Dómkirkja, is small but perfectly proportioned, with a plain wooden interior animated by glints of gold. (www.domkirkjan.is; Kirkjustræti; ⊙10am-4.30pm Mon-Fri, Mass 11am Sun)

# Eating

## Messinn                    SEAFOOD €€

9 🍴 MAP P40, D3

Make a beeline to Messinn for the best seafood that Reykjavík has to offer. The specialities here are the amazing pan-fried dishes: your pick of fish is served up in a sizzling cast-iron skillet, accompanied by buttery potatoes and salad. The mood is upbeat and comfortable and the staff friendly. (📞 546 0095; www.messinn.com; Lækjargata 6b; lunch mains 1850-2200kr, dinner mains 2700-4200kr; ⏲11.30am-3pm & 5-10pm; 🛜)

## Apotek                     FUSION €€

10 🍴 MAP P40, D2

This beautiful restaurant and bar with shining glass fixtures and a cool ambience is equally known for its delicious menu of small plates that are perfect for sharing and its top-flight cocktails. It's on the ground floor of the hotel of the same name. (📞 551 0011; www.apotekrestaurant.is; Austurstræti 16; mains 2800-6000kr; ⏲noon-11pm Sun-Thu, to midnight Fri & Sat)

## Grillmarkaðurinn           FUSION €€€

11 🍴 MAP P40, D3

Top-notch dining is the order of the day here, from the moment you enter the glass atrium with its golden-globe lights to your first snazzy cocktail, and on throughout the meal. Service is impeccable, and locals and visitors alike rave about the food, which uses Icelandic ingredients prepared with culinary imagination by master chefs. (Grill Market; 📞 571 7777; www.grillmarkadurinn.is; Lækjargata 2a; mains 3500-9500kr; ⏲11.30am-2pm & 6-10.30pm, closed Sat & Sun lunch)

## Fiskfélagið                SEAFOOD €€€

12 🍴 MAP P40, C2

The 'Fish Company' takes Icelandic seafood recipes and spins them through a variety of far-flung inspirations, from Fiji coconut to Spanish chorizo. Dine out on the terrace or in an intimate-feeling stone-and-timber room with copper light fittings and quirky furnishings. (📞 552 5300; www.fishcompany.is; Vesturgata 2a; mains lunch 2700-4600kr, dinner 4800-6600kr; ⏲11.30am-2.30pm & 5.30-10.30pm, closed Sat & Sun lunch)

## Fiskmarkaðurinn            SEAFOOD €€€

13 🍴 MAP P40, C2

Dramatic presentations of elaborate dishes fill the tables of this intimate, artistically lit restaurant, where chefs excel at infusing Icelandic seafood with Asian flavours such as lotus root. The tasting menu is acclaimed, and the place is renowned for its excellent sushi bar (3600kr to 4100kr). (Fishmarket; 📞 578 8877; www.fiskmarkadurinn.is; Aðalstræti 12; mains 4800-9900kr, tasting menu 11,900kr; ⏲5-10.30pm)

## Matarkjallarinn   ICELANDIC €€€

14  MAP P40, C2

Elegance is everywhere at Matarkjallarinn (the 'Food Cellar'). Brasserie-style dishes, Icelandic ingredients, magical decor and oh-so-skillful cocktails could draw you here. As could the slow-cooked cod, moss-cured salmon or smoked Arctic char. (☑558 0000; www.matarkjallarinn.is; Aðalstræti 2; mains lunch 2300-4000kr, dinner 4200-6500kr; ☺11am-3pm Mon-Fri, 5-11pm daily)

## Stofan Kaffihús   CAFE €

15  MAP P40, C2

In this historic brick building you'll find a warmly welcoming cafe with worn wooden floors, plump couches and a spacious main room. Settle in for coffee, cake or soup, and watch the world go by. Look out for the weekly board-game evenings for some retro fun. (☑546 1842; www.facebook.com/stofan.cafe; Vesturgata 3; dishes 1650-1900kr; ☺10am-10pm Sun-Wed, to midnight Thu-Sat; ☞)

## Café Kaffitár   CAFE €

16  MAP P40, A6

The ground-floor cafe at the National Museum offers wi-fi and a welcome respite, with wrap-around windows looking out on a flowing fountain. It serves a full range of coffee drinks as well as wholesome soups, sandwiches and salads. (Suðurgata 41; snacks 750-1900kr; ☺9am-5pm Mon-Fri, 10am-5pm Sat & Sun, closed Mon mid-Sep–Apr; ☞)

Stofan Kaffihús

### The City's Best Hot Dogs

Icelanders swear the city's best hot dogs are found at the **Bæjarins Beztu** (Map p40, D2; www.bbp.is; Tryggvagata; hot dogs 450kr; ☺10am-1am Sun-Thu, to 4.30am Fri & Sat) truck near the harbour (patronised by Bill Clinton and late-night bar-hoppers). Use the vital phrase 'eina með öllu' (one with everything) to get the quintessential favourite with sweet mustard, ketchup and crunchy onions.

### Icelandic Street Food

STREET FOOD €

17 ✖ MAP P40, D3

For a budget taste of old Iceland, squeeze into this tiny canteen that just loves showcasing home-cooked food. Owner Unnar has drafted in his grandmother to cook some of the dishes, which range from fish stew and lamb soup to rolled up pancakes dusted with sugar. Her principle that no one leaves her house hungry means free food refills. (☎691 3350; www.icelandicstreetfood.com; Lækjargata 8; mains from 1300kr; ☺8am-11pm)

### Icelandic Fish & Chips

SEAFOOD €€

Pick your fish and, voila, spelt-batter fried it becomes. Pair it with local beer, organic salads (990kr) and 'Skyronnaises' – *skyr*-based sauces (eg basil and garlic) that add a zing

to this most traditional of dishes. It's at Tryggvagata 11 (see 5 ☺ Map p40, C1). (☎511 1118; www.fishandchips.is; mains 1600-6300kr; ☺11.30am-9pm)

# Drinking

### Paloma

CLUB

18 ☺ MAP P40, C2

At one of Reykjavík's best late-night dance clubs DJs lay down reggae, electronica and pop upstairs, and a dark deep house dance scene in the basement. Find it in the same building as the Dubliner. (http://palomaclub.is; Naustin 1; ☺8pm-1am Thu & Sun, to 4.30am Fri & Sat)

### Loftið

COCKTAIL BAR

19 ☺ MAP P40, C2

Loftið is all about high-end cocktails and good living. Dress up to join the fray at this airy upstairs lounge, which features a zinc bar, retro tailor-shop-inspired decor, vintage tiles and a swank, older crowd. The basic booze here is top-shelf liquor elsewhere, and jazzy bands play from time to time. (Jacobsen Loftið; ☎551 9400; www.facebook.com/loftidbar; 2nd fl, Austurstræti 9; ☺4pm-1am Wed-Sat)

### Pablo Discobar

COCKTAIL BAR

20 ☺ MAP P40, C2

In the world's northernmost capital, Pablo Discobar offers an escape from darkness and disappointing weather for the price of a cocktail. Neon-bright and nostalgic, tropical-themed Pablo is Reykjavík's top stop for exotic drinks. Weekends bring DJ sets, Wednesday night brings deals on drinks. The bar also serves the downstairs tapas restaurant, Burro, until midnight. (📞552 7333; www.facebook.com/discobarrvk; Veltusundi 1; 🕐4pm-1am Sun-Thu, to 3am Fri & Sat)

### Skúli Craft Bar  CRAFT BEER

21 🚇 MAP P40, C2

The big draw here is the 14 craft beers on tap, the majority of which are normally Icelandic. Or you might want to opt for one of the bottled beers – there are around 130 brands to choose from (who's counting?). A six-beer flight costs 4500kr; happy hour is 4pm to 7pm. (📞519 6455; www.facebook.com/skulicraft; Aðalstræti 9; 🕐3-11pm Sun-Thu, to 1am Fri & Sat)

### Micro Bar  BAR

22 🚇 MAP P40, C2

Boutique brews are the name of the game at this low-key spot in the heart of the action. On tap you'll find 14 creations from the island's top microbreweries, and a happy hour (4pm to 7pm) of 900kr beers. Try the sampler trays of five mini draught beers for 3000kr (or 10 beers for 5000kr). (📞865 8389; www.facebook.com/MicroBarIceland; Vesturgata 2; 🕐3pm-midnight Sun-Thu, to 1am Fri & Sat)

### Frederiksen Ale House  PUB

23 🚇 MAP P40, C2

A modest selection of draught beers (happy hour is two-for-one; 4pm to 7pm) meets lots of bottled offerings and a decent pub-food menu, including brunch. Despite the address, you'll actually find the ale house on the junction of Tryggvagatta and Naustin. (📞571 0055; www.frederiksen.is; Hafnarstræti 5; 🕐11am-1am Mon-Sat, to 11pm Sun)

### Klaustur  WINE BAR

24 🚇 MAP P40, C3

One of Old Reykjavík's most beguiling night-time hideaways, low-key, welcoming Klaustur is primarily a wine bar, but drinks also include a bold selection of spirits, including the local Flóki malt whisky and smooth Katla vodka. (📞571 4421; www.klaustur.bar; Kirkjutorg 4; 🕐4pm-midnight Sun-Thu, to 2am Fri & Sat)

### Icelandic Craft Bar  CRAFT BEER

25 🚇 MAP P40, D3

A mellow hang-out with good views onto bustling Lækjargata and local brews including Einstök Arctic Ale on tap. The house beer is always 700kr (in Reykjavík this matters). (📞691 3350; www.facebook.com/icelandiccraftbar; Lækjargata 6; 🕐11am-1am Sun-Thu, to 3am Fri & Sat)

### Nightlife

Nightclubs in the Old Reykjavík quarter offer some of the city's best late-night DJ sets and intense dance scenes, but they start late – after midnight. To get deals on drinks, though, pop in early for happy hour, circling back to dance in the wee hours.

**Old Reykjavík** Drinking

# Entertainment

## Húrra

LIVE MUSIC

Dark and raw, this large bar opens up its back room to create a much-loved concert venue, with a wide range of live music or DJs on most nights. It's one of the best places in town to close out the evening. There's a range of beers on tap and happy hour runs till 9pm. You'll find it at Tryggvagata 22 (see 26 ⭐ Map p40, C2). (www.facebook.com/hurra.is; ⏰6pm-1am Mon-Thu, to 4.30am Fri & Sat, to 11.30pm Sun; 🛜)

## Gaukurinn

LIVE MUSIC

26 ⭐ MAP P40, C2

Grungy and glorious, Gaukurinn is a solid stop for live music, comedy, karaoke and open mikes. Happy hour is 7pm to 9pm. (www.gaukurinn.is; Tryggvagata 22; ⏰2pm-1am Sun-Thu, to 3am Fri & Sat)

## Nordic House

CULTURAL BUILDING

27 ⭐ MAP P40, XXX

This cultural centre fosters links between Iceland and its Nordic neighbours with a rich programme of events, a library, exhibition space and bistro. (Norræna Húsið;

## Icelandic Pop

Iceland's pop music scene is one of its great gifts to the world. Internationally famous Icelandic musicians include (of course) Björk and her former band, the Sugarcubes. Sigur Rós followed Björk to stardom; the concert movie *Heima* (2007) is a must-see. Indie-folk Of Monsters and Men stormed the US charts in 2011 with *My Head Is an Animal;* the band's latest album is *Beneath the Skin* (2015). Ásgeir had a breakout hit with *In the Silence* (2013), and *Afterglow* followed in 2017.

Reykjavík's flourishing music landscape is constantly changing – visit www.icelandmusic.is and www.grapevine.is for news and listings. Just a few examples of local groups include Seabear, an indie-folk band, which spawned top acts such as Sin Fang (*Flowers,* 2013; *Spaceland,* 2016) and Sóley (*We Sink,* 2012; *Ask the Deep,* 2015; *Endless Summer,* 2017). Árstíðir records minimalist indie-folk, and released *Verloren Verleden* with Anneke van Giersbergen in 2016.

Other local bands include pop-electronica act GusGus (*Lies Are More Flexible,* 2018), FM Belfast (*Island Broadcast,* 2017; electronica) and Múm (experimental electronica mixed with traditional instruments). Check out Singapore Sling for straight-up rock and roll, while dream-pop band Vök has won legions of local fans with its indie-electronica tunes. If your visit coincides with one of Iceland's many music festivals, go!

551 7030; www.nordichouse.is;
Sæmundargata 11; ⏰10am-5pm, to
9pm Wed; 🚌1, 3, 6, 12, 14)

### Iðnó Theatre

THEATRE

28 ⭐ MAP P40, XXX

Music and Icelandic theatre,
tending towards the comedic.
(📞537 8800; www.idnorvk.is;
Vonarstræti 3)

# Shopping

### Fischer

CONCEPT STORE

29 🔒 MAP P40, B2

Formally the recording studio of
Icelandic musician Jónsi, best
known as the Sigur Rós frontman,
this concept store feels like
walking through an immersive
exhibition. Perfumes, Icelandic
herbs, hand-crafted soap bars and
candles, ethereal music and visual
artwork play with all of the senses.
(www.fischersund.com; Fischersund 3;
⏰noon-6pm Mon-Sat)

### Kirsuberjatréð

ARTS & CRAFTS

30 🔒 MAP P40, C1

Talented designers show their
works at this long-running
women's art-and-design
collective. Highlights include the
bracelets and purses made from
soft, supple, brightly coloured
fish-skin leather, music boxes
made from string, and, our
favourite, beautiful coloured
bowls made from radish slices.
(Cherry Tree; 📞562 8990; www.kirs.
is; Vesturgata 4; ⏰10am-7pm Mon-
Fri, to 5pm Sat & Sun)

### Kolaportið Flea Market

Held in a huge industrial
building near the harbour,
**Kolaportið** (Map p40, D2;
www.kolaportid.is; Tryggvagata
19; ⏰11am-5pm Sat & Sun) is a
Reykjavík institution. There's
a vast tumble of second-hand
clothes, old toys and cheap
imports. A food section sells
traditional eats like *rúgbrauð*
(geothermally baked rye
bread).

### Akkúrat

DESIGN

31 🔒 MAP P40, C2

Browse the best of Nordic design,
from hand-painted mugs to
fisherfolk sweaters, at this concept
store supported by the **Iceland
Design Centre** (Hönnunarmiðstöð;
www.icelanddesign.is). Be sure to
check out the hats and sweaters
from local clothing brand Döðlur.
(📞868 7613; www.facebook.com/
akkuratreykjavik; Aðalstræti 2;
⏰10am-7pm Mon-Fri, to 6pm Sat,
11am-5pm Sun)

### Nordic Store

CLOTHING

32 🔒 MAP P40, D3

Ranks of traditional and
contemporary hand-knitted
*lopapeysur* (Icelandic woollen
sweaters), plus hats, headbands,
socks and gloves. (📞445 8080;
www.nordicstore.net; Lækjargata 2;
⏰9am-10pm)

# Explore ◎
# Old Harbour

*Largely service harbours until recently, the Old Harbour and neighbouring Grandi areas have blossomed into tourist hot spots, with key art galleries, museums, Northern Lights cinemas, eateries and shops. Whale-watching and puffin-viewing trips depart from the pier, and, as boat bells ding, photo ops abound with views of snow-capped Mt Esja and the Harpa concert hall.*

*Start by strolling the Old Harbour between whale-watching boats and wharfside restaurants. After a caffeine hit at Café Haiti (p61) it's on to the compelling Reykjavík Maritime Museum (p56). Next comes a street-food lunch at Grandi Mathöll (p58), then Omnom Chocolate (p56) and a mouth-watering (pre-booked) tour. Next stop: the Marshall House's three free galleries (p57); you can also order a cocktail here – by now it's happy hour. A waterside walk leads to epic pizza at Flatey (p58) or innovative Icelandic cuisine at Matur og Drykkur (p57). Still thirsty? The Bryggjan Brugghús microbrewery (p61) and Slippbarinn cocktail bar (p61) are both nearby.*

## Getting There & Around

🚶 A 1km walk from downtown, this compact, characterful neighbourhood is ripe for exploring on foot.

🚌 Strætó bus 14 runs to the Old Harbour from Laugardalur, via Hlemmur, the BSÍ terminal and Lækjartorg Sq in Old Reykjavík. Choose the Mýrargata stop for whale watching and Grandagarður for the Reykjavík Maritime Museum.

### Old Harbour Map on p54

## Top Experience 📷
# **Encountering Whales**

*Whale watching is a beloved pastime in Iceland, and boats depart year-round to catch glimpses of these magnificent beasts as they wave their fins, spout and dive. Northern waters around Húsavík and Akureyri are famous, but Reykjavík visitors can hop on a boat directly from the capital's Old Harbour. Trips are also tops for birdwatching.*

◉ **MAP P54, D6**

Tour tickets per 2-3hr trip from 9900kr, child from 4950kr

## Whales

The most common whales you'll spot on boats from Reykjavík are humpback whales (pictured left) and minke whales. The humpback is known for its curious nature and spectacular surface displays. The minke has a streamlined, slender, black body, a white striped pectoral fin and a tendency to leap entirely out of the water.

## Porpoises & Dolphins

Keep an eye out for tiny, shy harbour porpoises (*Phocoena phocoena*), which are easiest to spot in placid conditions. More gregarious white-beaked dolphins (*Lagenorhynchus albirostris*) often travel in larger pods and approach the boats year-round.

## Puffins & Seabirds

Bird life in Iceland is abundant, especially during the warmest months, when migrating species arrive to nest. You may see Arctic terns, gannets, guillemots and kittiwakes, but the stars of the show are the zippy, cutesy puffins.

## Tour Operators

**Elding Adventures at Sea** (☏ 519 5000; www.whalewatching.is; Ægisgarður 5; adult/child 11,000/5500kr; ☉ harbour kiosk 8am-9pm; ☒ 14) is the most established and ecofriendly outfit. Includes whale exhibition, angling and puffin-watching trips, as well as combo tours. Also runs the ferry to Viðey.

**Special Tours** (☏ 560 8800; www.specialtours.is; Ægisgarður 13; ☉ harbour kiosk 8am-8pm; ☒ 14) uses a small, fast boat for sea angling and whale watching. There are also puffin and combo tours.

**Whale Safari** (Mr Puffin; ☏ 497 0000; www.whalesafari.is; Ægisgarður 7; per passenger 22,000kr; ☉ harbour kiosk 8am-8pm mid-Apr–Oct; ☒ 14) offers whale-watching and puffin tours in a Zodiac.

## ★ Top Tips

o Make sure you book tours in advance.

o Trips are cancelled when sea conditions are foul.

o Tours generally run year-round, with more departures from May to August (prime viewing season).

o If you don't spot whales, many outfitters offer vouchers to come back and try again.

o Several companies also offer sea-angling (adult/child from 12,990/6500kr) and puffin-viewing trips (from 5700/2700kr), though you'll often see puffins while whale watching.

## ✖ Take a Break

Local institution Sægreifinn (p58) rustles up fresh fish grilled on skewers. A few steps away, Hamborgara Búllan (p59) dishes out legendary burgers.

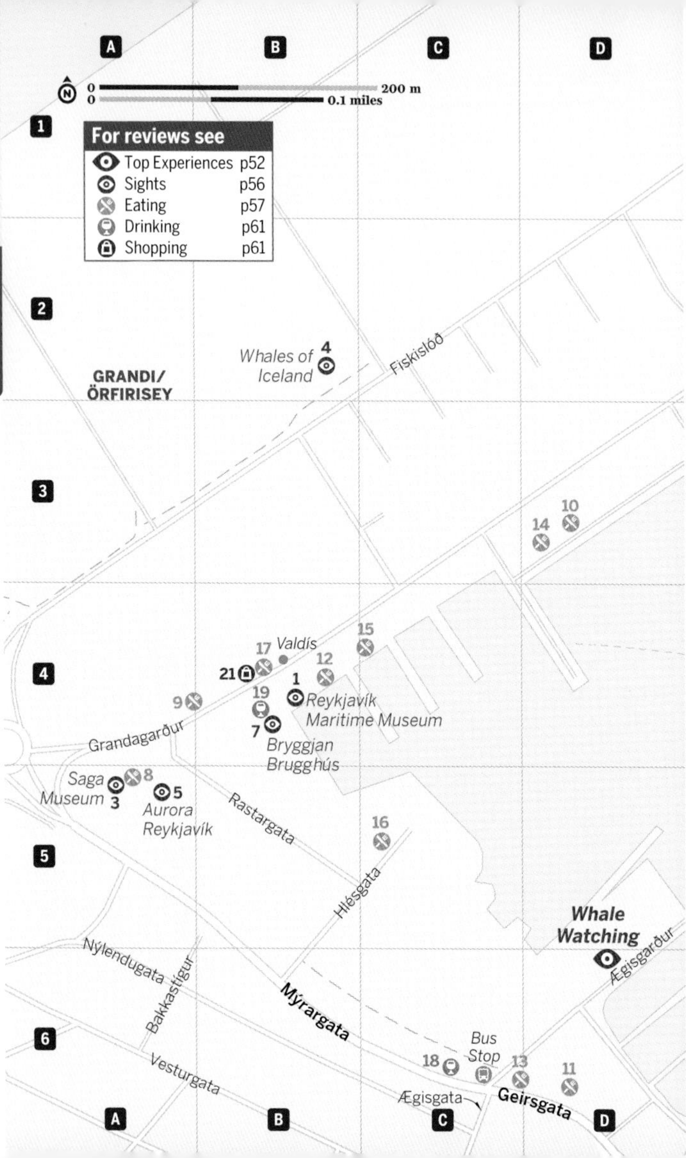

| A | B | C | D |

**1**

N 0 ————————— 200 m
0 ————————— 0.1 miles

**For reviews see**
- ◉ Top Experiences   p52
- ◉ Sights              p56
- ⊗ Eating             p57
- ⊖ Drinking          p61
- 🔒 Shopping         p61

**2**

GRANDI/
ÖRFIRISEY

*Whales of*  **4**
*Iceland* ◉

*Fiskislóð*

**3**

**10** ⊗

**14** ⊗

**4**

**17**  *Valdís*      **15** ⊗

**21**🔒         **12** ⊗

**9** ⊗   **19** ⊗  **1** ◉

**7** ◉  *Reykjavík*
*Maritime Museum*

*Bryggjan*
*Brugghús*

*Saga*  ⊗**8**
*Museum* ◉ ◉**5**
**3**  *Aurora*
*Reykjavík*

*Rastargata*

**5**

**16** ⊗

*Hlésgata*

*Nýlendugata*

**Whale**
**Watching**
◉
*Ægisgarður*

**6**

*Bakkastígur*

*Myrargata*

*Bus*
*Stop*

**18** ⊖  **13** ⊗   **11** ⊗

*Vesturgata*

*Ægisgata*

**Geirsgata**

| A | B | C | D |

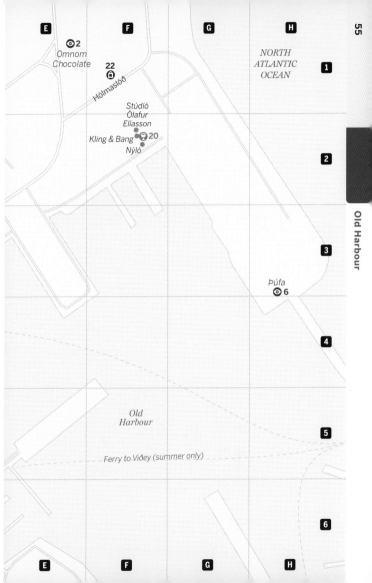

**E**

**◎2**
Omnom
Chocolate

**F**

**22**
🔒
Hólmaslóð

Stúdió
Ólafur
Elíasson

Kling & Bang ●◎20
Nýló ●

**G**

**H**

*NORTH*
*ATLANTIC*
*OCEAN*

**1**

**2**

**3**

Þúfa
**◎6**

**4**

*Old*
*Harbour*

*Ferry to Viðey (summer only)*

**5**

**6**

**E**    **F**    **G**    **H**

# Sights

## Reykjavík Maritime Museum
MUSEUM

1  MAP P54, B4

The crucial role fishing plays in Iceland's economy is celebrated through the imaginative displays in this former fish-freezing plant. The new exhibition Fish & folk evokes 150 years of the industry, using artefacts, sepia photos and interactive games to chart a course from the row boats of the late 1800s to the trawlers of the 21st century. Make time for one of the daily guided tours of the former coastguard ship Óðinn (1300kr). (Sjóminjasafnið í Reykjavík; 411 6300; www.maritimemuseum. is; Grandagarður 8; adult/child 1650kr/free, Óðinn & museum 2600kr; 10am-5pm, Óðinn tours at 11am, 1pm, 2pm & 3pm)

## Omnom Chocolate
FACTORY

2  MAP P54, E1

Reserve ahead for a tour (2pm Monday to Friday) at this full-service chocolate factory, where you'll see how cocoa beans are transformed into high-end, scrumptious delights. The shop sells its stylish bars (packaged with specially designed labels), which come in myriad sophisticated flavours. (519 5959; www.omnomchocolate.com; Hólmaslóð 4, Grandi; adult/child 3000/1500kr; 11am-6pm Mon-Fri, noon-4pm Sat)

## Saga Museum
MUSEUM

3  MAP P54, A5

The endearingly bloodthirsty Saga Museum is where Icelandic history is brought to life by eerie silicon models and a multi-language soundtrack featuring the thud of axes and hair-raising screams. Don't be surprised if you see some of the characters wandering around town, as moulds were taken from Reykjavík residents (the owner's daughters are the Irish princess and the little slave gnawing a fish). (511 1517; www.sagamuseum. is; Grandagarður 2; adult/child 2200/800kr; 10am-6pm)

## Whales of Iceland
MUSEUM

4  MAP P54, B2

Ever strolled beneath a blue whale? This museum houses full-sized models of the 23 species of whale found off Iceland's coast. The largest museum of this type in Europe, it also displays models of whale skeletons, and has good audio guides and multimedia screens to explain what you're seeing. There's a cafe and gift shop too. (571 0077; www.whalesof iceland.is; Fiskislóð 23; adult/child 2900/1500kr; 10am-5pm)

## Aurora Reykjavík
MUSEUM

5  MAP P54, A5

Learn about the classical tales explaining the Northern Lights, and the scientific explanation, then watch a 35-minute pano-ramic, high-definition recreation

## Marshall House: Art Galleries & Studios

Once a fish-meal factory, now home to three innovative arts spaces – the restoration of the Marshall House is a key factor in Grandi's rise as an arty enclave. It's also home to Marshall (p61), a cool bar.

**Nýló** (Nýlistasafnið – The Living Art Museum; Map p54, F2; ☑ 551 4350; www.nylo.is; Grandagarður 20, Marshall Húsið, Grandi; admission free; ☉ noon-6pm Tue, Wed & Fri-Sun, to 9pm Thu) A dynamic centre for emerging and established contemporary artists, live music and other performances.

**Kling & Bang** (Map p54, F2; ☑ 554 2003; http://this.is/klingandbang; Grandagarður 20, Marshall Húsið, Grandi; admission free; ☉ noon-6pm Wed & Fri-Sun, to 9pm Thu) A perennially cutting-edge, artist-run exhibition space that's a favourite with locals.

**Stúdíó Ólafur Elíasson** (Map p54, F2; ☑ 551 3666; www.olafureliasson.net; Grandagarður 20, Marshall Húsið, Grandi; admission free; ☉ noon-6pm Tue, Wed & Fri-Sun, to 9pm Thu) Internationally acclaimed Icelandic-Danish artist Ólafur Elíasson was responsible for the Harpa concert hall's iconic facade. Expect big installations, perhaps of driftwood, ribboning metal and textured light.

of Icelandic auroras. (Northern Lights Centre; ☑ 780 4500; www.aurorareykjavik.is; Grandagarður 2; adult/child 1600/1000kr; ☉ 9am-9pm)

## Þúfa

SCULPTURE

6 ◉ MAP P54, H3

Þúfa (th-oo-fha), meaning 'the Tussock', was created by artist Ólöf Nordal in 2013. The 8m-tall grassy mound was constructed out of 4500 tons of gravel and is one of the biggest artworks ever made in Iceland. It's crowned by the type of hut that's used to make harðfiskur (dried fish). Þúfa is set at the harbour mouth in the Grandi area and offers fine views of the Old Harbor and Faxa Bay. (Norðurslóð)

## Bryggjan Brugghús

BREWERY

7 ◉ MAP P54, B4

The 30-minute tours of the gleaming vats at this waterfront microbrewery come with either a three- or six-beer tasting flight. Tours leave on the hour; there's no need to book. (☑ 456 4040; www.bryggjanbrugghus.is; Grandagarður 8; tours 3500-5000kr; ☉ noon-10pm)

# Eating

## Matur og Drykkur

ICELANDIC €€

8 ◉ MAP P54, A5

One of Reykjavík's top high-concept restaurants, Matur og Drykkur means 'Food and Drink', and you'll surely be plied with the best of both. The brainchild of chef

CAROLYNE PARENT/SHUTTERSTOCK ©

Grandi Mathöll

Gísli Matthías Auðunsson, who also owns the excellent Slippurinn (p114), it creates inventive versions of traditional Icelandic fare. Book ahead in high season and for dinner. (☎571 8877; www.maturogdrykkur.is; Grandagarður 2; lunch/dinner mains from 1900/3400kr, tasting menu 10,000kr; ⏱11.30am-3pm & 6-10pm, closed Sun lunch; ☝)

## Flatey Pizza  PIZZA €

9 ❌ MAP P54, A4

Flatey raises pizza making to something akin to an art form. Its sourdough circles are made from organic wheat and are baked for just one minute at 500°C to keep the toppings tasty. It's very hip and very classy. As you can't book, be prepared to queue. (☎588 2666; www.flatey.pizza; Grandagarður 11; pizzas 1750-2650kr; ⏱11am-10pm)

## Grandi Mathöll  STREET FOOD €

10 ❌ MAP P54, D3

There's no neater encapsulation of Grandi's rejuvenation than the transformation of this old fish factory into a pioneering street-food hall. Long trestle tables sit beside stalls selling a diverse range of lamb, fish and veggie delights; look out for the Gastro Truck, its succulent signature chicken burger has quite a jalapeño kick. (☎577 6200; www.grandimatholl.is; Grandagarður 16; mains from 1200kr; ⏱11am-9pm Mon-Thu, to 10pm Fri-Sun)

### Sægreifinn SEAFOOD €

11  MAP P54, D6

Sidle into this green harbourside shack for the most famous lobster soup in the capital. Though the original sea baron sold the restaurant some years ago, the place retains its unfussy charm. (Seabaron; 553 1500; www.saegreifinn.is; Geirsgata 8; mains from 1500kr; 11.30am-10pm)

### Messinn Granda SEAFOOD €€

12 MAP P54, B4

Sample the catch of the day at this buffet-style harbour restaurant, serving its freshly caught selection on steaming skillets with root vegetables and spinach. The simple preparation was developed at Messinn's popular saloon-sized downtown restaurant (p44). ( 546 0095; www.messinn.com; Grandagarður 8; lunch/dinner buffet 2300/5000kr; lunch 11.30am-2pm, dinner 6-10pm)

### Hamborgara Búllan BURGERS €

13 MAP P54, C6

This outpost of burgerdom and Americana proffers savoury patties that are perennial local favourites. Hollywood film stars have been known to come here to feed too. (Hamborgarabúlla Tómasar; 511 0800; www.bullan.is; Geirsgata 1; burgers/meals from 1300/2000kr; 11.30am-9pm; )

### Bergsson RE SEAFOOD €€

14 MAP P54, D3

An acclaimed seafood spot with harbour views and a daily-changing lunch menu featuring the freshest catch. The same family runs Bergsson Mathús (p37) in Old Reykjavík. ( 571 0822; www.bergsson.net; Grandagarður 16; mains 1500-2600kr; 9am-4pm Mon-Fri)

### Kaffivagninn DINER €€

15 MAP P54, C4

A harbourside eatery with broad windows looking onto the bobbing boats. There are good breakfasts and hearty seafood-based lunches. ( 551 5932; www.kaffivagninn.is; Grandagarður 10; mains 1600-3000kr; 7.30am-9pm Mon-Fri, from 9am Sat & Sun; )

### Fish & Chips SEAFOOD €

16 MAP P54, C5

Delicious, piping-hot fish and chips are on offer at this simple food truck near the Víkin Maritime Museum. (www.fishandchipsvagninn.is; Hlésgata; mains 1200-2200kr; 11am-9pm)

## Ice Cream! 🍽

Interestingly for such a chilly country, Icelanders love their ice cream. Throughout the summer, happy families flock to **Valdís** (Map p54, B4; 586 8088; www.valdis.is; Grandagarður 21; scoops 490kr; 11.30am-11pm; ), take a number and join the crush waiting for a scoop of homemade delight.

# Ethics & Eating

Many Icelandic restaurants tout dishes such as whale *(hvál/hvalur)*, shark (fermented and called *hákarl*) and puffin *(lundi)*. Before ordering, consider that what may have been sustainable with 350,000 Icelanders becomes taxing on species and ecosystems when 2.2 million tourists annually (more than six times the population) get involved. Be aware of the following:

○ As much as an estimated 60% of Icelandic whale-meat consumption is by tourists.

○ A 2017 Gallup survey found that 81% of Icelanders had never eaten whale meat. And only 1% of Icelanders questioned said they eat whale regularly.

○ Fin whales are classified as endangered globally; their status in the North Atlantic region is hotly debated.

○ Iceland's Ministry of Industries & Innovation (www.government.is) maintains that the whale catch is sustainable (at less than 1% of local stocks), is strictly managed and is in accordance with international law.

○ The International Fund for Animal Welfare (www.ifaw.org) claims that recent campaigns have helped halve whale-meat consumption by tourists, with more than half the restaurants in downtown Reykjavík pledging not to serve it.

○ The Greenland shark, which is used for *hákarl,* has a conservation status of 'near threatened' globally.

○ Recent studies suggest Greenland shark might have a lifespan of some 500 years, but are only able to reproduce after 150 years, making the species slow to recover from any reduction in numbers.

○ Iceland's iconic Atlantic puffin is classified as a vulnerable species globally because of rapid European population decline.

○ Since 2003 there's been a drop in the puffin population of about 40%.

While we feature restaurants serving these meats in our listings, you can opt not to order it, or find whale-free spots at www.icewhale.is/whale-friendly-restaurants.

## 17 Sortir BAKERY €

17 ✕ MAP P54, B4

From Toblerone cupcakes and vegan pastries to four-layer chocolate cake – the daily selection here includes something for every sweet tooth. The name '17 Sortir' refers to a diligent housewife in a novel by Nobel Prize–winner Halldór Laxness who believed offering 17 types of cake was the bare minimum when guests arrived. (📞571 1701; www.sautjansortir.is; Grandagarður 19; ⏱10am-6pm Mon-Fri, 11am-5pm Sat & Sun)

# Drinking

## Slippbarinn COCKTAIL BAR

18 🍸 MAP P54, C6

Jet-setters unite at this buzzy bar at the Icelandair Hotel Reykjavík Marina. It's bedecked with vintage record players and cool locals sipping some of the best cocktails in town. For cut-price creations drop by during happy hour (3pm to 6pm). (📞560 8080; www.slippbarinn.is; Mýrargata 2; ⏱noon-midnight Sun-Thu, to 1am Fri & Sat; 🛜)

## Bryggjan Brugghús CRAFT BEER

19 🍺 MAP P54, B4

Cavernous, dimly lit and dotted with vintage pub paraphernalia, harbourside Bryggjan Brugghús is a roomy microbrewery where 12 taps dispense its own fresh-tasting beers. Join one of the regular brewery tours (p57) then settle back to sip a house beer – 600kr during happy hour (3pm to 7pm). (📞456 4040; www.bryggjanbrugghus.is; Grandagarður 8; ⏱11am-midnight Sun-Thu, to 1am Fri & Sat; 🛜)

## Marshall BAR

20 🍺 MAP P54, F2

The perfect pit stop for art aficionados, Marshall sits in the same building as three cutting-edge galleries. It's appropriately aesthetically appealing: an industrial-chic spot with coppery colours, a beautiful backlit bar and great city views. (📞519 7766; www.marshallrestaurant.is; Grandagarður 20, Marshall Húsið, Grandi; ⏱11.30am-11pm Tue-Sun; 🛜)

# Shopping

## Steinunn CLOTHING

21 🔒 MAP P54, B4

Browse the couture collection of celebrated Icelandic designer Steinunn Sigurðardóttir, featuring innovative knitwear. (📞588 6649; www.steinunn.com; Grandagarður 17; ⏱11am-6pm Mon-Fri, 1-4pm Sat)

## Farmers & Friends CLOTHING

22 🔒 MAP P54, F1

Gorgeous boots, clothes and accessories in earthy tones fill the shelves of this design company's store. The emphasis is firmly on natural fabrics and materials. (Farmers Market; 📞552 1960; www.farmersmarket.is; Hólmaslóð 2; ⏱10am-6pm Mon-Fri, 11am-5pm Sat & Sun)

# Explore

# Laugavegur & Skólavörðustígur

*Reykjavík's main street for shopping and people-watching is bustling, often-pedestrianised Laugavegur. The narrow, one-way lane and its side streets blossom with the capital's most interesting shops, cafes and bars. At its western end, its name changes to Bankastræti, then Austurstræti. Running uphill off Bankastræti, artists' street Skólavörðustígur ends at the spectacular modernist Hallgrímskirkja.*

*Breakfast at Grái Kötturinn (p76), then cross the street to explore Icelandic art and heritage at the Culture House (p72). Marvel at iconic Harpa (p72), then get lost in Icelandic landscapes at the Reykjavík Art Museum – Kjarvalsstaðir (p72). After eating organic at Gló (p76), zip to the top of Hallgrímskirkja (p64) for views. Next, either the lakeside National Gallery of Iceland (p72) or a dip in the geothermal pools at Sundhöllin (p72). Reserve ahead to dine at Dill (p74), SKÁL! (p74) or Nostra (p75). Or opt for cool street eats at Hlemmur Mathöll (p75) or pizza at Hverfisgata 12 (p75). Perhaps take in an Icelandic flick at Bíó Paradís (p79) before hitting the bars.*

## Getting There & Around

🚶 Within the neighbourhood it's easiest to walk, as many of the roads are one-way or pedestrianised.

🚌 Buses 1, 3, 6, 11, 12 and 13 run between the key Hlemmur bus stop at the eastern end of Laugavegur, through to central Lækjartorg Sq, before continuing onward.

**Laugavegur & Skólavörðustígur Map on p70**

## Top Experience 📷

# Gawk at Hallgrímskirkja

*Reykjavík's soaring white-concrete church dominates the city skyline and is visible from 20km away. The graceful church was named after poet Reverend Hallgrímur Pétursson (1614–74), who wrote Iceland's most popular hymn book, Passion Hymns. The church's size and radical design caused controversy, and its architect, Guðjón Samúelsson (1887–1950), never saw its completion – it took 41 years (1945–86) to build.*

◎ MAP P70, D6

☏ 510 1000

www.hallgrimskirkja.is

Skólavörðustígur

tower adult/child 1000/100kr

🕑 9am-9pm May-Sep, to 5pm Oct-Apr

## Facade & Tower

The columns on either side of the church's signature 74.5m-high tower represent volcanic basalt, part of architect Guðjón Samúelsson's desire to create a national architectural style. Get a spectacular panorama of the city by taking an elevator trip up the tower, where you'll find great photo ops from the viewing area.

## Organ

In contrast to the high drama outside, the Lutheran church's interior is quite plain. The most eye-catching feature is the vast, gleaming 5275-pipe organ, installed in 1992. It was made in Germany by Johannes Klais Orgelbau and individuals sponsored each of the pipes; their names are inscribed on them. Towards the altar, you'll find the quaint older organ, still in use.

## Concerts & Services

From mid-June to late August, hear half-hour **choir concerts** (www.scholacantorum.is; 2500kr) at noon on Wednesday, and **organ recitals** (www.listvinafelag.is) at noon on Thursday and Saturday (2000kr), and for one hour on Sunday at 5pm (2500kr). Services are held on Sunday at 11am, with a small service on Wednesday at 8am. There is an English service on the last Sunday of the month at 2pm.

## Leifur Eiríksson Statue

At the front, gazing proudly into the distance, is a statue of the Viking Leifur Eiríksson (pictured left), the first European to discover America. A present from the USA on the 1000th anniversary of the Alþingi (Parliament) in 1930, it was designed by Alexander Stirling Calder (1870–1945), the father of the perhaps more famous, modern mobilist and sculptor Alexander Calder (1898–1976).

★ **Top Tips**

○ Try for a local's pronunciation: Hallgrímskirkja is pronounced *hatl-krims-kirk-ya*.

○ There are occasional rotating art exhibitions in the church's foyer.

○ Check online for the schedule of organ and choral recitals during your visit.

✕ **Take a Break**

Cross the street to **ROK** (Map p70, D5; ☏ 544 4443; www.rokrestaurant.is; Frakkastígur 26a; dishes 1300-2400kr; ⏱ 11.30am-11pm) for small tapas-style plates of Icelandic fare.

Head down Skólavörðustígur to a plethora of eateries; try classic Kaffi Mokka (p78), Reykjavík's oldest coffee shop, for a light meal.

# Walking Tour 🥾

## Reykjavík Art & Design

*Icelanders have a knack for piquant, arresting art and design. The city is littered with local creations, including modernist architecture, cool contemporary art, and shops full of functional but creative crafts and design gadgets. This walk takes you through a sampling of the disciplines, all in a compact, popular section of central Reykjavík.*

**Start** Reykjavík Art Museum – Kjarvalsstaðir

**End** Harpa

**Length** 3km; two hours

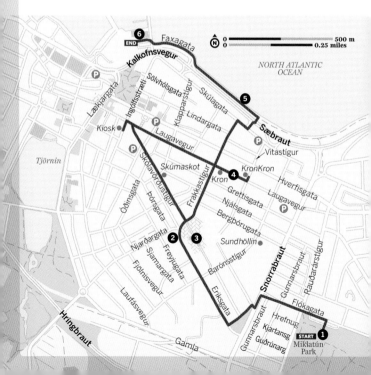

## ❶ Reykjavík Art Museum – Kjarvalsstaðir

The Kjarvalsstaðir (p72) looks onto Miklatún Park, and is named for Jóhannes Kjarval (1885–1972), one of Iceland's most popular classical artists. The peaceful museum displays his evocative landscapes and also the works of many major 20th-century Icelandic painters.

## ❷ Einar Jónsson Museum

Einar Jónsson (1874–1954) was one of Iceland's foremost sculptors, with his dramatic allegorical style. The Einar Jónsson Museum (p74) fills the studio he designed. Upper stories have city views; the **sculpture garden** (www.lej.is; Freyjugata; ◷24hr) behind it is free.

## ❸ Hallgrímskirkja

Guðjón Samúelsson (1887–1950), perhaps Iceland's most renowned 20th-century architect, created a distinctive Icelandic aesthetic. Hallgrímskirkja (p64) is possibly the pinnacle of his work. Pop around the corner to classic 1937 swimming pool Sundhöllin (p72), to see another example.

## ❹ Design Shops

Icelandic artists and designers create many objects that combine beauty and practicality. The streets here are loaded with shops selling designers' work. Kron (p80) and KronKron

## ✖ Take a Break

Stop for a delicious, organic meal at Gló (p75), where the menu changes daily and is accompanied by a broad bar of intricate and flavourful salads. A colourful crew of locals crowds in for popular lunches, and plenty of bars and coffee shops sit just nearby.

(p79), on Laugavegur, have top clothes and wild and wonderful shoes. Skúmaskot (p80), on Skólavörðustígur, is packed with unique handmade art and clothing, and at Kiosk (p80), at Ingólfsstræti 6, you'll find a couture cooperative.

## ❺ Art

Walk to the ocean's edge for the popular *Sun Voyager* (Sólfar; p73) sculpture. It was created by Jón Gunnar Árnason, and its skeletal, shiplike frame sits powerfully along the water, with snow-topped mountains in the distance.

## ❻ Harpa

Reykjavík's dazzling Harpa concert hall (p72), with its facade of glimmering hexagons, opened in 2011 and was designed by Danish firm Henning Larsen Architects, Icelandic firm Batteríið Architects and Danish-Icelandic artist Olafur Eliasson. Be sure to zip inside to see its vaulted glass panels and wonderful harbour sightlines.

# Walking Tour 🥾

## Djammið Nightlife

*Reykjavík is renowned for its wild, wonderful party scene. Called djammið (meaning going out on the town), the high-spirited nightlife is at its most colourful on weekends: many cafes and bistros transform into raucous beer-soaked bars, joining the dedicated pubs and clubs. But it's not the quantity of drinking dens that makes Reykjavík's nightlife special – it's the crowd's upbeat energy).*

**Start** Kaldi
**End** Prikið
**Length** 400m

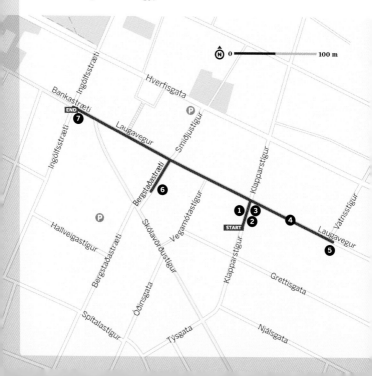

## ❶ Warming Up

Start the night at **Kaldi** (📞581 2200; www.kaldibar.is; Laugavegur 20b; ⏰noon-1am Sun-Thu, to 3am Fri & Sat) and enjoy a beer. Effortlessly cool with mismatched seats and teal banquettes, plus a popular smoking courtyard, Kaldi carries the full range of its own microbrews. Anyone can play the piano.

## ❷ Time to Dance

Next go to **Kiki** (www.kiki.is; Laugavegur 22; ⏰8pm-1am Wed, Thu & Sun, to 4.30am Fri & Sat). Ostensibly a gay bar, this is also the place to get your dance on, since much of Reykjavík's nightlife centres on the booze, not the groove. If you can squeeze beneath the flamingo sign and beyond the rainbow-striped tin siding, you'll find one of Reykjavík's best dance parties.

## ❸ Enjoy a Beer

Or you can go next door to **Bravó** (Laugavegur 22; ⏰11am-1am Mon-Thu, to 3am Fri, & Sat). Its claim to have the city's longest happy hour (11am to 8pm, local draught beer 800kr) isn't its only asset, you'll also find friendly bartenders, great people watching, cool tunes on the sound system and a laid-back vibe.

## ❹ Strolling Laugavegur

By now you should be feeling the *djammið* vibe; it's a perfect time to simply stroll packed Laugavegur, people-watching and striking up conversations. This may be the moment where you toss guidebook routes and

just roll with the locals: pubs and late-night bars abound throughout the centre.

## ❺ Rock Out!

Next, head down the street for beer, beards and the odd flying bottle...atmospheric **Dillon** (📞697 6333; www.dillon.is; Laugavegur 30; ⏰noon-1am Sun-Thu, to 3am Fri & Sat) is a RRRROCK pub with a great beer garden. Frequent loud, live bands hit its tiny corner stage. Get dark and get sweaty.

## ❻ The Beautiful People

The old house with the London Underground symbol over the door contains one of Reykjavík's coolest bars: **Kaffibarinn** (📞551 1588; www.kaffibarinn.is; Bergstaðastræti 1; ⏰3pm-1am Sun-Thu, to 4.30am Fri & Sat; 📶). It had a starring role in the cult movie *101 Reykjavík* and, at weekends, its so busy you may need a famous face or a battering ram to get in.

## ❼ Staggering Home

The atmosphere at one of Reykjavík's oldest joints, **Prikið** (📞551 2866; www.prikid.is; Bankastræti 12; ⏰8am-1am Mon-Thu, to 4.30am Fri, 11am-4.30am Sat, 11am-1am Sun), falls somewhere between diner and saloon, though it usually gets dancey in the wee hours. If you're still standing and you're longing for some greasy eats before heading home, tuck into burgers or the popular next-day 'hangover killer' breakfast. Or grab a fresh pizza slice at the **Deli** (www.deli.is; Bankastræti 14), just up the block.

Old Harbour

**1**
Harpa

Faxagata

Geirsgata

Kalkofnsvegur

Geirsgata

Skúlagata

Naustin

Sæbraut

Tryggvagata

Ingólfsstræti

Sölvhólsgata

Skúlagata

**2** Vínbúðin –
Austurstræti

Austurstræti

Lækjargata

Lindargata

Lækjartorg Sq

**2**
Culture
House

Posthússtræti

Nordic
Store

**36** **24**

**23** **10**

Smiðjustig

Veghst

**20**

**OLD
REYKJAVÍK**

Amtmannsst

Skólastræti

Þingholtsstræti

Ingólfsstræti

Grái
Kötturinn

Laugavegur

Klapparstígur

Hverfisgata

**34**

Bókhlöðust

Kaffi
Mokka

**25**

**15**
**35**

Vatnsstígur

**27**

Tjörnin

Laufásvegur

Miðst

Hallveigastígur

Bergstaðastræti

Reykjavík
Record Shop

**22**

**26** **16**

**3**

Frikirkjuvegur

Spítalast

**33**

**28**

12 Tónar

**38**

**17**

Bakarí
Sandholt

Grettisgata

**29**

Handknitting
Association
of Iceland

**32**

Njálsgata

Brauð
& Co

**3**
National
Gallery of
Iceland

Þingholtsstræti

Bjargarst

Grundarst

Bergstaðastræti

Freyjugata

Lokastígur

Skólavörðustígur

Þórsgata

Bjarnarst

Reykjavík
Roasters

Hallargarðurinn

Hellus

Óðinsgata

Karastígur

Skothúsvegur

Baldursgata

Baldursgata

**13**

Bragagata

Frakkastígur

Sóleyjargata

Fjölugata

Lautásvegur

Bergstaðastræti

Nönnugata

Urðarst

Frjólnisvegur

Njarðargata

Sjamargata

**Hallgrímskirkja**

Einar Jónsson
Museum

**8**

Eiríksgata

Freyjugata

**9**

Mimisvegur

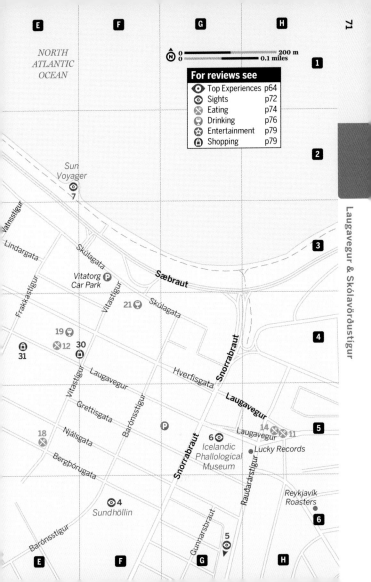

Laugavegur & Skólavörðustígur

NORTH
ATLANTIC
OCEAN

N 0 ——————— 200 m
0 ——————— 0.1 miles

**For reviews see**
◉ Top Experiences p64
◉ Sights p72
✖ Eating p74
🍷 Drinking p76
★ Entertainment p79
🔒 Shopping p79

Sun
Voyager
◉ 7

Vatnsstígur
Lindargata
Skúlagata
Frakkastígur
Vítastígur

Vitatorg P
Car Park

Sæbraut

Skúlagata
21 🍷

19 🍷
✖ 12  30
🔒
🔒 31

Laugavegur
Grettisgata
Vítastígur
Barónsstígur

Hverfisgata

Snorrabraut

Laugavegur

18 ✖
Njálsgata
Bergþórugata

P

Snorrabraut

6 ◉
Icelandic
Phallological
Museum

14 ✖ ✖ 11
Laugavegur
● Lucky Records

Reykjavík
Roasters

◉ 4
Sundhöllin

Barónsstígur

Gunnarsbraut

5 ◉

Raudarárstígur

6

# Sights

## Harpa

ARTS CENTRE

1 ◎ MAP P70, C1

With its ever-changing facets glistening on the water's edge, Reykjavík's sparkling Harpa concert hall and cultural centre is a beauty to behold. In addition to a season of top-notch shows (some free), the shimmering interior with harbour vistas is worth stopping in for, or take a highly recommended, 30-minute guided tour (1500kr). Tours run two to three times daily year-round, with up to eight daily between mid-June and mid-August. ( ☎ box office 528 5050; www.harpa.is; Austurbakki 2; ⏱ 8am-midnight, box office noon-6pm)

## Culture House

GALLERY

2 ◎ MAP P70, C2

This fantastic collaboration between the National Museum, National Gallery and four other organisations creates a superbly curated exhibition covering the artistic and cultural heritage of Iceland from settlement to today. Priceless artefacts are arranged by theme, and highlights include 14th-century manuscripts, contemporary art, and the skeleton of a great auk (now extinct). Check the website for free guided tours. (Þjóðmenningarhúsið; ☎ 530 2210; www.culturehouse.is; Hverfisgata 15; adult/child incl National Museum 2000kr/free; ⏱ 10am-5pm daily May–mid-Sep, closed Mon mid-Sep–Apr)

## National Gallery of Iceland

MUSEUM

3 ◎ MAP P70, A4

This pretty stack of marble atriums and spacious galleries overlooking Tjörnin offers ever-changing exhibits drawn from a 10,000-piece collection. The museum can only exhibit a small sample at any one time; shows range from 19th- and 20th-century paintings by Iceland's favourite artists (including Jóhannes Kjarval and Nína Sæmundsson) to sculptures by Sigurjón Ólafsson and others. (Listasafn Íslands; ☎ 515 9600; www.listasafn.is; Fríkirkjuvegur 7; adult/child 1800kr/free; ⏱ 10am-5pm daily mid-May–mid-Sep, 11am-5pm Tue-Sun mid-Sep–mid-May)

## Sundhöllin

GEOTHERMAL POOL

4 ◎ MAP P70, F6

Our top pick for a Reykjavík city-centre swim. Sundhöllin reopened in 2017 after a year-long revamp that added an entire outdoor area with hot tubs, sauna and a swimming pool. The original indoor pool remains open, as well as the secret upstairs hot tub with excellent city views. (Sundhöll Reykjavíkur; ☎ 411 5350; www.reykjavik.is/stadir/sundholl-reykjavikur; Barónsstígur 16; adult/child 950/150kr; ⏱ 6.30am-10pm Mon-Fri, from 8am Sat & Sun; ♿)

## Reykjavík Art Museum – Kjarvalsstaðir

GALLERY

5 ◎ MAP P70, G6

The angular glass-and-wood Kjarvalsstaðir, which looks out

onto **Miklatún Park**, is named for Jóhannes Kjarval (1885–1972), one of Iceland's most popular classical artists. He was a fisherman until his crew paid for him to study at the Academy of Fine Arts in Copenhagen, and his wonderfully evocative landscapes share space alongside changing installations of mostly Icelandic 20th-century paintings. (📞411 6420; www.artmuseum.is; Flókagata 24, Miklatún Park; adult/child 1650kr/free; ⏱10am-5pm)

### Icelandic Phallological Museum

MUSEUM

6 ◉ MAP P70, G5

Oh, the jokes are endless here... This unique museum houses a huge collection of penises, and it's actually very well done. From pickled pickles to petrified wood,

there are 286 different members on display, representing all Icelandic mammals and beyond. Featured items include contributions from sperm whales and a polar bear, silver castings of each member of the Icelandic handball team and a single human sample – from deceased mountaineer Páll Arason. (Hið Íslenzka Reðasafn; 📞561 6663; www.phallus.is; Laugavegur 116; adult/child 1500kr/free; ⏱10am-6pm, from 9am Jun-Aug)

### Sun Voyager

SCULPTURE

7 ◉ MAP P70, E2

Reykjavík has some fascinating sculptures, but it's Jón Gunnar Árnason's shiplike *Sun Voyager* (*Sólfar*) sculpture that seems to catch visitors' imaginations. Scooping in a skeletal arc along

Harpa

NIC LEHOUX ©

## Combined Tickets

○ The Reykjavík Art Museum ticket covers all three of its sites.

○ A joint ticket for the National Gallery, nearby Ásgrímur Jónsson Collection and further-afield Sigurjón Ólafsson Museum costs 1800kr.

the seaside, it offers a photo shoot with snowcapped mountains in the distance. (Sæbraut)

### Einar Jónsson Museum
GALLERY

8 🔘 MAP P70, D6

Einar Jónsson (1874–1954) is one of Iceland's foremost sculptors, famous for intense symbolist works. Chiselled representations of Hope, Earth and Death burst from basalt cliffs, weep over naked women and slay dragons. Jónsson designed the building, which was built between 1916 and 1923, when this hill was on the outskirts of town. It also contains his austere penthouse flat and studio. (📞551 3797; www.lej.is; Eiriksgata 3; adult/child 1000kr/free; ⊙10am-5pm Tue-Sun)

### Ásgrímur Jónsson Collection
GALLERY

9 🔘 MAP P70, B6

Iceland's first professional painter, Ásgrímur Jónsson (1876–1958) was the son of a farmer. He lived and worked here, and you can visit his former atelier to see his work, which incorporates folk tales and

Icelandic nature. (📞515 9625; www.listasafn.is; Bergstaðastræti 74; adult/child 1000kr/free; ⊙1-5pm daily mid-May–early Sep, 2-5pm Sat & Sun early Sep-Nov & Feb–mid-May)

# Eating

### Dill
ICELANDIC €€€

10 🍴 MAP P70, B3

Exquisite 'New Nordic' cuisine is the major drawcard at Reykjavík's elegant Michelin-starred bistro. Skilled chefs use a small number of ingredients to create highly complex dishes in a parade of courses. The owners are friends with Copenhagen's famous Noma clan and take Icelandic cuisine to similarly heady heights. It's hugely popular; book well in advance. (📞552 1522; www.dillrestaurant.is; Hverfisgata 12; 5/7 courses 11,900/13,900kr; ⊙6-10pm Wed-Sat)

### SKÁL!
STREET FOOD €

11 🍴 MAP P70, H5

SKÁL! demands your attention – with its capital lettering and punctuation but most emphatically with its food. Experimental offerings combine unusual flavours (fermented garlic, birch sugar, Arctic thyme salt) with Icelandic ingredients to impressive effect, best sampled at a stool beside its neon-topped bar. There's an excellent list of vegan creations and the cocktails feature foraged herbs. (📞775 2299; www.skalrvk.com; Hlemmur Mathöll, Laugavegur 107; mains 1000-2500kr; ⊙noon-10pm Sun-Wed, to 11pm Thu-Sat; 🌱)

## Nostra
NEW NORDIC €€€

12  MAP P70, E4

Fine-dining Nostra is where fresh, local ingredients – à la New Nordic Cuisine – are turned into French-inspired multicourse tasting menus, including those for vegans, vegetarians and pescatarians. Nostra refers to its menus as 'experiences' and with their intense flavours and picture-perfect presentation, it's not wrong. (☑ 519 3535; www.nostrarestaurant.is; Laugavegur 59; 4/6/8 courses 8900/11,900/13,900kr; ☻ 5.30-10pm Tue-Sat; 🖉)

## Þrír Frakkar
ICELANDIC, SEAFOOD €€€

13  MAP P70, B5

Owner-chef Úlfar Eysteinsson has built up a consistently excellent reputation at this snug little restaurant. Specialities range throughout the aquatic world from salt cod and halibut to *plokkfiskur* (fish stew) with black bread. Non-fish items run towards guillemot, horse, lamb and whale. (☑ 552 3939; www.facebook.com/3frakkar.is; Baldursgata 14; mains 4200-6250kr;

11.30am-2.30pm & 6-10pm Mon-Fri, 6-11pm Sat & Sun)

## Hlemmur Mathöll
FOOD HALL €

14  MAP P70, H5

If only all bus terminals had a food court like this. Some 10 vendors rustle up multicultural foods, including Danish *smørrebrød* (rye bread), Mexican tacos and Vietnamese street food. The pick is innovative SKÁL! Most stalls kick into action by lunchtime. (www.hlemmurmatholl.is; Laugavegur 107; mains from 800kr; ☻ 8am-11pm)

## Gló
ORGANIC, VEGETARIAN €

15  MAP P70, C3

Join the cool cats in this airy upstairs restaurant serving fresh daily specials loaded with Asian-influenced herbs and spices. Though not exclusively vegetarian, it's a wonderland of raw and organic foods, with a broad bar of elaborate salads. (☑ 553 1111; www.glo.is; Laugavegur 20b; mains 1000-2400kr; ☻ 11.30am-10pm; 🛜 🖉)

---

### Brilliant Bakeries
🍽️

Prepare to take sides in the battle for Reykjavík's best bakery. **Bakarí Sandholt** (Map p70, D4; ☑ 551 3524; www.sandholt.is; Laugavegur 36; snacks 700-2700kr; ☻ 7am-7pm Sun-Thu, 6.30am-9pm Fri & Sat; 🛜) is usually crammed with folks hoovering up the assortment of fresh baguettes, croissants, pastries and sandwiches. The soup of the day comes with delicious sourdough bread. Or queue for some of the city's best home-baked breads and pastries at **Brauð & Co** (Map p70, D4; www.braudogco.is; Frakkastígur 16; ☻ 6am-6pm Mon-Fri, to 5pm Sat & Sun), where you can watch Viking hipsters make the goodies while you wait.

## Public House

FUSION, TAPAS €€

16  MAP P70, D4

Excellent Asian-style tapas and great local draught beers are just part of the draw at this gastropub. It's also a fun place to hang out, with its pounding pop soundtrack and no less than *two* happy hours (3pm to 6pm and 11pm to 1am). ( 555 7333; www. publichouse.is; Laugavegur 24; small plates 1100-2500kr; 11.30am-11pm, bar to 1am)

## Joylato

ICE CREAM €

17  MAP P70, C4

Scoops of high-end homemade ice cream and sorbets in delectable flavours, including Icelandic strawberries. (www.joylato.is; Njálsgata 1; scoops from 650kr; noon-10pm)

### Brunch with Björk?

Blink and you'll miss **Grái Kötturinn** (Map p70, C3; 551 1544; www.facebook.com/graikot turinn; Hverfisgata 16a; mains 1100-2500kr; 7.15am-2pm Mon-Fri, 8am-2pm Sat & Sun), a tiny six-table cafe and favourite of Björk. It looks like a cross between an eccentric bookshop and an art gallery, and serves toast, bagels, pancakes, and bacon and eggs on freshly baked bread.

## Vitabar

BURGERS €

18  MAP P70, E5

Sidle up to the bar for your short-order burger with some of the best hand-cut fries you'll find. This is a tile-and-formica kind of joint, with American rock on the stereo and locals quaffing pints of cold Einstök and Viking. (Bergþórugata 21; mains 900-3400kr; 11.30am-11pm, bar to 1am or 2am Fri & Sat)

# Drinking

## Kaffi Vínyl

CAFE

19  MAP P70, E4

'Vegan is the new black' reads the neon sign, vinyl discs spin on the decks and a cool crowd tucks into meat-free noodles, burgers and pasta (mains from 1400kr). Happy hour lasts from 4pm to 7pm. ( 537 1332; www.facebook.com/ kaffivinyl; Hverfisgata 76; 8am-11pm Sun-Thu, to 1am Fri & Sat; )

## Port 9

WINE BAR

20  MAP P70, D3

Port 9 sauntered onto Reykjavík's drinking scene supremely confident in the quality of its wines and the knowledge of its staff – offerings here range from affordable tipples by the glass to vintages to break the bank. Low lighting, an arty clientele and a secret hang-out vibe (it's tucked down a tiny street) make it worth tracking down. ( 832 2929; www. facebook.com/portniu; Veghúsastígur 7; 4-11pm Tue-Sat, to 9pm Sun & Mon)

## KEX Bar

BAR

21 MAP P70, F4

Locals love this hostel bar-restaurant in an old cookie factory (*kex* means 'biscuit') for its broad sea-view windows, inner courtyard and own-brew beer. Happy hipsters soak up the 1920s Vegas vibe: saloon doors, old-school barber station, happy chatter and scuffed floors. Look out for regular, free, live jazz sessions. (Sæmundur í Sparifötunum; www.kexhostel.is; Skúlagata 28; 11.30am-11pm; )

## Bravó

BAR

22 MAP P70, D4

What's claimed to be the city's longest happy hour (11am to 8pm, local draught beer 800kr) isn't Bravó's only asset. You'll also find friendly bartenders, great people watching, cool tunes on the sound system and a laid-back vibe. (Laugavegur 22; 11am-1am Mon-Thu, to 3am Fri & Sat; )

## Loft Hostel Bar

BAR

23 MAP P70, B3

On sunny days locals pack the roof terrace at this lively patio bar at the hostel of the same name. Happy hour (4pm to 7pm) also draws a crowd. (www.lofthostel.is; Bankastræti 7; noon-11pm)

## Petersen Svítan

LOUNGE

24 MAP P70, B3

The sweeping roof terrace at this lounge-bar at the top of a restored old theatre is supremely stylish, with decking, rattan sofas

Kaffi Vínyl

EGILL BJARNASON/LONELY PLANET ©

Laugavegur & Skólavörðustígur Drinking

## The Cafe Scene

The city's ratio of coffee houses to citizens is staggering. The folks at **Reykjavík Roasters** (Map p70, D5; ☎517 5535; www.reykjavikroasters.is; Kárastígur 1; ⏰7am-6pm Mon-Fri, 8am-5pm Sat & Sun) take their coffee seriously, and it's the first stop for local coffee aficionados. It also has a sunny **branch** (Map p70, H6; ☎552 3200; Brautarholt 2; ⏰8am-5.30pm Mon-Fri, 9am-5pm Sat & Sun; 🛜) in the Hlemmur area. Or soak up the vibe at Reykjavík's oldest coffee shop, **Kaffi Mokka** (Map p70, C3; ☎552 1174; www.mokka.is; Skólavörðustígur 3a; ⏰9am-6.30pm, to 9pm Jun-Aug), where little has changed since the 1950s, from its original mosaic pillars and copper lights to its waffles, sandwiches and coffees.

and expansive views. It's one of the hottest spots in town when the sun shines. (Gamla Bíó; ☎563 4000; www.gamlabio.is; Ingólfsstræti 2a; ⏰noon-1am Sun-Thu, to 3am Fri & Sat)

### Bastard
CRAFT BEER

25 ⭐ MAP P70, C3

Bastard's in-house microbrewery produces two beers for the taps here and around a dozen others sit alongside. It's a swish spot, with an upbeat soundtrack and a buzzy vibe. Happy hour is from 4pm to 7pm. (☎558 0800; www.bastard.is; Vegamótastígur 4; ⏰11.30am-1am Sun-Thu, to 4am Fri & Sat)

### Veður
BAR

26 ⭐ MAP P70, D4

Cosily cool Veður has a beautifully lit bar, welcoming vibe, acclaimed cocktails and a long happy hour (noon to 7.30pm). (www.vedurbarinn.is; Klapparstígur 33; ⏰noon-1am Sun-Thu, to 3am Fri & Sat)

# Entertainment

### Bíó Paradís
CINEMA

27 ⭐ MAP P70, D3

This totally cool cinema, decked out in movie posters and vintage officeware, screens specially curated Icelandic films with English subtitles and international flicks. It's a chance to see movies that you may not find elsewhere. (☎412 7711; www.bioparadis.is; Hverfisgata 54; adult 1600-1800kr; 🛜)

### Mengi
LIVE PERFORMANCE

28 ⭐ MAP P70, C4

It may be small, but Mengi offers an innovative program of music and visual and performing arts. (☎588 3644; www.mengi.net; Óðinsgata 2; ⏰noon-5pm Tue-Sat & for performances)

### Hannesarholt

LIVE MUSIC

29 ⭐ MAP P70, B4

Cafe and intimate music venue in the house of former prime minister, Hannes Hafstein, in 1915 –catch intimate classical pianists or opera singers here. (📞511 1904; www.hannesarholt.is/english/; Grundarstígur 10)

# Shopping

### KronKron

CLOTHING

30 🔒 MAP P70, F4

This is where Reykjavík goes high fashion, with labels such as Marc Jacobs and Vivienne Westwood. But we really enjoy its Scandinavian designers

(including Kron by KronKron) and the offering of silk dresses, knit capes, scarves and even woollen underwear. The handcrafted shoes are off the charts; they are also sold down the street at Kron. (📞561 9388; www.kronkron.com; Laugavegur 63b; ⏰10am-6pm Mon-Fri, to 5pm Sat)

### Kron

SHOES

31 🔒 MAP P70, E4

Kron sells its own outlandishly wonderful handmade shoes with all the flair you'd expect of an Icelandic label. Colours are bright, textures are cool, and they're even wearable (those practical Icelanders!). (📞551 8388; www.kron.is; Laugavegur 48; ⏰10am-6pm Mon-Fri, to 5pm Sat)

Reykjavík Shopping

Kaffi Mokka

## Skúmaskot
ARTS & CRAFTS

**32** MAP P70, C4

Local designers create unique porcelain items, women's and kids' clothing, paintings and cards. It's in a large, renovated gallery that beautifully showcases the creative Icelandic crafts. (663 1013; www.facebook.com/skumaskot. art.design; Skólavörðustígur 21a; 10am-6pm Mon-Fri, to 5pm Sat, noon-4pm Sun)

## Rammagerðin
GIFTS & SOUVENIRS

**33** MAP P70, C4

One of the city's better souvenir shops, Rammagerðin offers loads of woollens, crafts and collectibles. It also has branches at Skólavörðustígur 20, Banka-stræti 9 and Keflavík International

### Sweaters & Knitted Goods

If you're hankering for some of the local knitwear, the **Handknitting Association of Iceland** (Handprjónasamband Íslands; Map p70, C4; 552 1890; www.handknit.is; Skólavörðustígur 19; 9am-10pm Mon-Fri, to 6pm Sat, 10am-6pm Sun) sells traditional hats, socks and sweaters; you can also buy yarn, needles and knitting patterns.

Nordic Store (p49) sells loads of hand- or machine-made *lopapeysur* (sweaters) and other wool products from it's base in Old Reykjavík.

Airport. (Iceland Gift Store; 535 6690; www.icelandgiftstore.com; Skólavörðustígur 12; 10am-9pm)

## Kiosk
CLOTHING

**34** MAP P70, B3

This wonderful designers' cooperative is lined with creative women's fashion in a glass-fronted boutique. Designers take turns staffing the store. (571 3636; www.kioskreykjavik.com; Ingólfsstræti 6; 11am-6pm Mon-Fri, to 5pm Sat)

## Mál og Menning
BOOKS

**35** MAP P70, C3

A friendly, well-stocked independent bookshop with a strong selection of English-language books offering insights to Iceland. It also sells maps, CDs, games and newspapers and has a good cafe (soup and bread 1000kr). (580 5000; www.bmm.is; Laugavegur 18; 9am-10pm Mon-Fri, 10am-10pm Sat; )

## 66° North
CLOTHING

**36** MAP P70, B3

Iceland's premier outdoor-clothing company began by making all-weather wear for Arctic fishers. This metamorphosed into costly, fashionable streetwear: jackets, fleeces, hats and gloves. Friendly staff can explain the different materials and their uses to help you make an educated choice. It has another city-centre store at Laugavegur 17. (535 6680; www.66north.is; Bankastræti 5; 9am-8pm Mon-Sat, 10am-8pm Sun)

## Icelandic Record Shops

**Lucky Records** (📞551 1195; www.luckyrecords.is; Rauðarárstígur 10; 🕙10am-6pm Mon-Fri, 11am-5pm Sat & Sun) holds an eclectic array of modern Icelandic music, plenty of vintage vinyl too and stages occasional live music.

**12 Tónar** (📞511 5656; www.12tonar.is; Skólavörðustígur 15; 🕙10am-6pm Mon-Sat, from noon Sun) has launched some of Iceland's favourite bands; it's two-floor shop is a very cool place to hang out: listen to CDs, drink coffee and sometimes catch a gig. Or, scratch your vinyl itch at the central

**Reykjavík Record Shop** (📞561 2299; www.facebook.com/reykjavik recordshop; Klapparstígur 35; 🕙11am-6pm Mon-Fri, 1-6pm Sat).

## Dogma
CLOTHING

37 🔒 MAP P70, D4

This quirky T-shirt specialist is the go-to spot for scouting out funky local designs with a cartoonish appeal. It also does a nice line in comic fridge magnets and drink coasters that gently mock the tourist trade. It has another branch in the Kringlan mall. (Reykjavík T-Shirts; 📞562 6600; www.dogma.is; Laugavegur 32; 🕙10am-8pm Jun-Sep, to 6pm Oct-May)

## Orrifinn
JEWELLERY

38 🔒 MAP P70, C4

Orrifinn's subtle, beautiful jewellery captures the natural wonder of Iceland and its Viking history. Delicate anchors, axes and pen nibs dangle from understated matte chains. There are some workbenches here so you're likely to see the jewellers creating pieces. (📞789 7616; www.orrifinn. com; Skólavörðustígur 17a; 🕙10am-6pm Mon-Fri, 11am-4pm Sat)

# Worth a Trip 🔭

# Laugardalur

*The park at Laugardalur, 4km east of the centre, was once the main source of Reykjavík's hot water: Laugardalur means 'Hot Springs Valley', and you'll still find relics from the old wash house. The area is a favourite with locals for its huge geothermal swimming complex, spa, arenas, skating rink, botanical gardens, cafe, and kids' zoo and entertainment park. Nearby there are top museums and a farmers market.*

## Getting There

🚌 2, 5, 14, 15 and 17 pass 200m from Laugardalur park; 14 is closest to the pool. Bus 16 serves the waterfront and Sigurjón Ólafsson Museum.

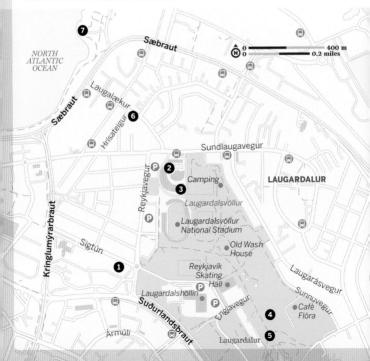

## ❶ Local Art

Visit Ásmundur Sveinsson's playful sculptures at Reykjavík Art Museum's **Ásmundarsafn** (Ásmundur Sveinsson Museum; ☎411 6430; www.artmuseum.is; Sigtún; adult/child 1650kr/free; ⏰10am-5pm May-Sep, 1-5pm Oct-Apr). Monumental concrete creations fill the garden, while inside are works in wood, clay and metals. Visit the dome: acoustics create the museum's 'must-sing policy'.

## ❷ Hot Springs

Reykjavík's naturally hot water is the heart of the city's social life. **Laugardalslaug** (☎411 5100; www.reykjavik.is/stadir/laugardalslaug; Sundlaugavegur 30a; adult/child 950/150kr, suit/towel rental 850/570kr; ⏰6.30am-10pm Mon-Fri, 8am-10pm Sat & Sun; 👶) has the largest, best facilities: Olympic-sized pools, a string of hot-pots, saltwater tub, steam bath and a curling 86m water slide.

## ❸ Workout & Pampering

**Laugar Spa** (☎553 0000; www.laugarspa.com; Sundlaugavegur 30a; day pass 5800kr; ⏰6am-11pm Mon-Fri, 8am-9.30pm Sat & Sun) offers six saunas and steam rooms, a sea-water tub, a gym, fitness classes, a cafe, and beauty and massage clinics. The spa is 18+ and includes access to Laugardalslaug.

## ❹ Gourmet Gardens

The **Reykjavík Botanic Gardens** (Grasagarður; ☎411 8650; www.grasagardur.is; admission free; ⏰10am-10pm May-Sep, to 3pm Oct-Apr) contain over 5000 varieties of subarctic plant species, seasonal flowers and bird life, and a wonderful summer cafe, **Café Flóra** (Flóran; ☎553 8872; www.floran.is; cakes from 950kr; mains 1550-3150kr; ⏰8am-10pm May-Sep; 🚶).

## ❺ Family Fun

The **Reykjavík Zoo & Family Park** (Fjölskyldu og Húsdýragarðurinn; ☎411 5900; www.mu.is; adult/child 880/660kr, 1/10 ride ticket 330/2520kr; ⏰10am-6pm Jun–mid-Aug, to 5pm mid-Aug–May) gets packed with happy local families. Don't expect lions; think seals, foxes and farm animals. The family park section has a mini-racetrack, child-size bulldozers, a giant trampoline, boats and rides.

## ❻ Shop Local

**Frú Lauga** (☎534 7165; www.frulauga.is; Laugalækur 6; ⏰10am-6pm Mon-Fri, to 4pm Sat) farmers market sources its products from all over the countryside. Sample *skyr* desserts from Erpsstaðir farm, organic vegetables, meats, wine and the like.

## ❼ Waterfront Sculpture & Walks

The peaceful seafront studio of sculptor Sigurjón Ólafsson (1908–82) is now the **Sigurjón Ólafsson Museum** (Listasafn Sigurjóns Ólafssonar; ☎553 2906; www.lso.is; Laugarnestanga 70; adult/child 1000kr/free; ⏰1-5pm daily mid-May–mid-Sep, 2-5pm Sat & Sun mid-Sep–Nov & Feb–mid-May), showcasing his powerful busts and driftwood totem poles.

## Worth a Trip 🔭

# Viðey

*On fine-weather days, the tiny uninhabited island of Viðey (www.videy.com) makes a wonderful day trip. You can enjoy occasional cultural tours with varying themes in summer, while in late August some Reykjavikers come to pick wild caraway. Less than 1km off Reykjavík's Skarfabakki harbour, it feels a world away. Surprising modern artworks, an abandoned village and great birdwatching add to its remote spell.*

## Getting There

⛴ Ferries depart from Skarfabakki year-round (weekends only in winter), and Harpa and the Old Harbour in summer.

🚌 Bus 16 stops at Skarfabakki, on the City Sightseeing bus route.

# 1 Viðeyarstofa & Church

Skúli Magnússon (1711–94), the powerful sheriff, built Viðeyarstofa as his home here in the 1750s. Now it houses a **cafe** (mains 2450-3900kr; 11.30am-5pm mid-May–Sep, 1.30-4pm Sat & Sun Oct–mid-May; ) serving basic fare such as burgers and waffles. Explore the adjacent 18th-century wooden church with Skúli's tomb.

# 2 Local History

Viðey was settled around AD900 and farmed until the 1950s. It was home to a powerful monastery from 1225, but in 1539 it was wiped out by Danish soldiers during the Reformation. Look for the remains of the **monastery** behind the Viðeyarstofa.

# 3 Explore the Island

The whole island is criss-crossed with **walking paths**. Some you can bicycle, others are more precarious. A good map at the harbour shows which are which. The island is great for **birdwatching** (30 species breed here) and **botany** (over one-third of all Icelandic plants grow on the island).

# 4 Bike It

In summer you can hire a bike at the Old Harbour at **Reykjavík Bike Tours** (694 8956; www.icelandbike.com; Ægisgarður 7; bike rental per 4hr from 3500kr; 9am-5pm Jun-Aug, shorter hours Sep-May) and bring

it with you on the ferry. There's nothing quite like the free, wind-in-your-hair feeling of cycling along the island paths.

# 5 Check Out the Art

Visit Yoko Ono's **Imagine Peace Tower** (2007), a 'wishing well' that blasts a dazzling column of light into the sky every night between 9 October (John Lennon's birthday) and 8 December (the anniversary of his death). For information on Peace Tower tours from Reykjavík, see www.videy.com.

# 6 Barbecue

Locals in the know come prepared with cook-out supplies and head to glass-fronted **Viðeyjarnaust** day-hut, on a beautiful headland, which has a public barbecue.

# 7 To the North

Trails leading northwest take you around ponds, past some monuments to shipwrecks, the low cliffs of **Eiðisbjarg**, and **Vesturey** at the northern tip of the island. Richard Serra's huge basalt sculptures, **Áfangar** (Standing Stones; 1990), dot this part of the island.

# 8 Southern Ruins

Trails to the southeast lead past the natural sheepfold **Réttin**, the tiny grotto **Paradíshellir** (Paradise Cave) and then to the abandoned fishing village at **Sundbakki**.

## Top Experience 📷
# Get Wet at the Blue Lagoon

*In a magnificent black-lava field, 47km southwest of Reykjavík, this milky-teal spa is fed by water (at a perfect 38°C) from the futuristic Svartsengi geothermal plant. Those who say it's too commercial aren't wrong, but the colour and feel of the water is truly otherworldly, and with the roiling steam clouds and people daubed in white mud, you'll feel like you're on another planet.*

Bláa Lónið

📞 420 8800

www.bluelagoon.com

Nordurljosavegur 9

adult/child from 7000kr/free, premium entry from 9600kr/free

## A Good Soak

The super-heated spa water (70% sea water, 30% fresh water) is rich in blue-green algae, mineral salts and fine silica mud, which condition and exfoliate the skin. It sounds like advertising speak, but you really do come out as soft as a baby's bum.

## Explore the Complex

The complex includes eateries, a rooftop viewpoint and a shop; the pool boasts hot-pots, steam rooms, a sauna, a floating noodle station, a silica-mask station, a bar and a piping-hot waterfall delivering a powerful hydraulic massage that's like being pummelled by a troll. A VIP section has its own wading space, lounge and viewing platform.

## Massage

For extra relaxation, lie on a floating mattress and have a massage therapist knead your knots (30/60 minutes 10,000/16,000kr). Book spa treatments well in advance.

## Opening Hours

The Blue Lagoon is open from 8am to 10pm January to late May and mid-August to September, 7am to 11pm late May to June, 7am to midnight July to mid-August, and from 8am to 9pm from October to December.

## Stay Longer

The uber-luxurious **Retreat Hotel** (☏420 8800; www.bluelagoon.com/accommodation/retreat-hotel; Norðurljósavegur 9; r from 140,600kr; P❄�🛜🏊) has floor-to-ceiling windows overlooking the mineral blue waters. The **Blue Lagoon – Silica Hotel** (☏420 8800; www.bluelagoon.com/accommodation/silica-hotel; Norðurljósavegur 7; d incl breakfast from 54,000kr; P@🛜🏊) and **Northern Light Inn** (☏426 8650; www.northernlightinn.is; d incl breakfast from 28,000kr; P@🛜) are also both nearby.

★ **Top Tips**

o Pre-book or be turned away.

o Get e-tickets from the website or vouchers from tour firms.

o If you're taking a tour, check whether you need to book lagoon tickets separately.

o Avoid summertime between 10am and 2pm. Go early or after 7pm.

o Luggage checks (550kr per bag, per day) enable to/from airport stops.

o Thorough, naked pre-pool showering is standard practice.

★ **Getting There**

o Reykjavík Excursions (www.re.is) runs frequent bus services from Reykjavík and the airport.

✕ **Take a Break**

**Blue Café** (snacks 850kr, sandwiches 1200kr; 🛜) offers cafeteria-style eats. **LAVA Restaurant** (mains lunch/dinner 4500/5900kr; 🛜) has high-end Icelandic dishes.

# Worth a Trip 🔭

# Reykjanes Peninsula

The Reykjanes Peninsula (www.visitreykjanes.is) is special not only for the Blue Lagoon, Iceland's most famous attraction, but for other local favourites. Sweet fishing hamlets Garður and Sandgerði sit minutes from the airport. Untamed landscapes of volcanic craters, mineral lakes, hot springs and rugged, ATV-ready mountains and coastal lava fields stretch from Reykjanestá to the Reykjanesfólkvangur Wilderness Reserve.

## Getting There

🚗 Best way to travel.

🚌 From Keflavík town, Strætó (www.bus.is) bus 89 serves Garður and Sandgerði, bus 55/1 goes to Reykjavík and 88 connects to Grindavík.

## ❶ Garður

Garður's beautiful windswept **Garðskagi headland** is great for birdwatching and sometimes seal or whale spotting. Two quaint lighthouses add drama. There's a small folk museum, too.

## ❷ Local History & Seafood

In Sandgerði, take time to look at the fascinating exhibit about shipwrecked explorer Jean-Baptiste Charcot at the **Sudurnes Science and Learning Center** (☎ 423 7551/5; www.thekkingarsetur. is; Garðskagavegur; adult/child 6-15 years 600/300kr, child under 6 years free; ⏱ 10am-4pm Mon-Fri, 1-5pm Sat & Sun May-Sep, 10am-2pm Mon-Fri Oct-Apr). Enjoy a seafood lunch at excellent **Vitinn** (☎ 423 7755; www. vitinn.is; Vitatorg 7; mains 2700-6900kr; ⏱ 11.30am-2pm & 6-9pm Mon-Sat).

## ❸ Birds & Bards

Pleasant **beaches** dot the coast south of Sandgerði, and the surrounding marshes are frequented by more than 190 species of birds. You'll find a lonely church at **Hvalsnes**, featured in a famous Icelandic hymn by Hallgrímur Pétursson (1616–74), written at the death of his young daughter, who was buried here.

## ❹ Crossing Continents

The **Bridge Between Two Continents** (Negur) sees you traversing a rift created when the North American and Eurasian tectonic plates shifted. They drift further apart by around 2cm a year – you get to walk across the 18m bridge or stand in the canyon below.

## ❺ Valahnúkur

One of the most wild and wonderful spots on the peninsula is the lava fields at Valahnúkur. Dramatic cliffs and the **Reykjanesviti lighthouse** sit near a multicoloured geothermal area with hot spring **Gunnuhver**.

## ❻ Break in Grindavík

For a late-afternoon pick-me-up, stop off at charming dock-front cafe **Bryggjan** (☎ 426 7100; www. facebook.com/bryggjancafegrindavik; Miðgarður 2; cakes/sandwiches 850/ 1000kr, soup 1700-2000kr; ⏱ 8am-10pm Mon-Fri; 🛜), in Grindavík.

## ❼ Open Air

To explore Reykjanes by foot or ATV, Grindavík is home to outfitters **ATV Adventures** (4x4 Adventures Iceland; ☎ 857 3001; www.4x4adventuresiceland. is; Tangasund). The **tourist office** (☎ 420 1190; www.visitgrindavik.is; Hafnargata 12; ⏱ 10am-5pm mid-May– mid-Sep) stocks walking-trail maps.

## ❽ Springs, Lava & Lakes

Looping back to Reykjavík, visit either the Blue Lagoon (p86), late, like the locals, or the dramatic lava, hot springs and lakes around the 300-sq-km **Reykjanesfólkvangur Wilderness Reserve**.

# Southwest Iceland's Regions

## Borgarnes & Around (p133)
Welcome to 'Sagaland', a region rich in wild tales of Iceland's Viking past, where you'll hike deep into ice caves before soaking in chic geothermal spas.

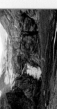

**Snæfellsjökull National Park**

**Settlement Centre**

**Þingvellir National Park**

**Gullfoss**

**Geysir**

**Jökulsárlón**

## South Coast (p109)
On this cinematic shore, puffins perch on sea stacks, waterfalls thunder down cliffs, and glacial tongues meet icy lagoons.

## Snæfellsnes Peninsula (p123)
This bewitching blend of photogenic mountains, black-sand beaches and horse farms also offers whale watching, glacial hikes and lava tubes.

## Golden Circle (p93)
Iceland in a day: gushing cascades at glittering Gullfoss, Geysir's spurting geyser and Þingvellir's mighty fissures and tectonic plates. Plus volcanoes, hot springs and geothermal pools.

# Explore
# Southwest Iceland

*The beautiful Southwest has many of Iceland's legendary natural wonders: black-sand beaches stretch along the Atlantic, geysers spout from geothermal fields and waterfalls glide across escarpments while brooding volcanoes and glittering ice caps score the inland horizon.*

## Worth a Trip 🔭

# Explore ◎

# Golden Circle

*Diving in glacial waters, absorbing the grandeur of the first-ever parliamentary site and watching the earth belch boiling water 30m high – the Golden Circle has it all. The 300km route features three knockout sights: Þingvellir, where tectonic plates meet; Geysir, where water erupts more than 100 times a day; and the roaring and staggeringly voluminous waterfall Gullfoss.*

*Get an early start from Reykjavík and head to Þingvellir (p96), spending at least an hour wandering the parliament site, rift and falls. En route, visit the Gljúfrasteinn Laxness Museum (p102), home of Nobel Prize–winning author Halldór Laxness. Lunch at Efstidalur II (p103) on local fish and burgers; don't miss the farm ice cream. Then visit Geysir and Strokkur (p98), and Gullfoss (p94). If time permits, squeeze in river rafting near Reykholt (p104). Spend your evening at Gamla Laugin (p101), a historic geothermal pool next to meadows and a rushing brook. Afterwards, dine on fine Icelandic fare at romantic Tryggvaskáli (p104), in Selfoss.*

## Getting There & Around

🚗 The Golden Circle is very easy to drive on your own.

🚌 'Iceland On Your Own' (one daily mid-June to early September) from Reykjavík Excursions links Reykjavík with Geysir (4800kr one way) and Gullfoss (5000kr). No regular buses currently run to Þingvellir. You can also choose from myriad bus tours.

### Golden Circle Map on p100

Gamla Laugin (p101), Flúðir JEAFISH PING/SHUTTERSTOCK ©

## Top Experience 📷
# **Feel the Roar at Gullfoss**

*Dropping into the canyon of the Hvítá river, Gullfoss (Golden Falls) is a key stop on Golden Circle tours. It's made up of two cascades: the first drop is 11m and the second is 21m, through which around 38 million tonnes of water charge on a daily basis. The sheer volume of water here is a sight to behold.*

◉ MAP P100, E1

www.gullfoss.is

Rte 35/Kjalvegur

admission free

## Views & Photo Ops

A tarmac path leads from the main parking lot and visitor centre to a grand **lookout** over the falls. Stairs then continue down to the level of the falls. Alternatively, drive in on the spur below the tourist centre at falls-level for disabled-accessible parking. A path then continues down the valley towards the thundering falls for the most captivating video shots.

## Saving the Falls

Sigríður Tómasdóttir (1871–1957) and her sisters made the first stairs to the falls, guiding people through formerly impassable terrain. In 1907 foreign investors wanted to dam the Hvítá river, which feeds the falls, for a hydroelectric project. Sigríður's father, Tómas Tómasson, only leased them the land, but the developers got permission from the government. Sigríður walked (barefoot!) to Reykjavík to protest. When the investors failed to pay the lease, the agreement was nullified and the falls escaped destruction. Gullfoss was donated to the nation, and since 1979 it's been a nature reserve. Look for the **memorial** to Sigríður near the foot of the stairs from the visitors centre.

## Nearby: the Kjölur Route

Gullfoss is the final stop on traditional Golden Circle tours. You can continue along magnificent Rte F35 beyond the falls (the Kjölur route) for 14.8km while it's paved, after which you need to have a 4WD. Alternatively, take a Highland-routed 'Iceland On Your Own' bus service (17,900kr) with **Reykjavík Excursions** (☏ 580 5400; www.ioyo.is), which also stops at the Kerlingarfjöll hiking area (8300kr one way).

### ★ Top Tips

○ On grey days mist can obscure the second drop, making Gullfoss slightly less spectacular.

○ Don't step over the barriers – they're there not just to protect you, but also the fragile environment.

○ There's accommodation a few kilometres before the falls at **Hótel Gullfoss** (☏ 486 8979; www.hotelgullfoss.is; Brattholt; d incl breakfast 20,000kr; 🛜), where clean en suite rooms overlook the moors (get one facing the valley), and there are two hot-pots and a restaurant (mains 2500kr to 4900kr) with sweeping views.

### ✕ Take a Break

Above Gullfoss and next to the main parking lot, the tourist information centre has a **cafe** (Kjalvegur/Rte 35; menu items from 990kr; ⏱ 9am-9pm Jun-Aug, to 6.30pm Sep-May; 🛜) that sells lamb soup, salads, sandwiches, cakes and coffee.

Top Sights 📷

# Walk Through History at Þingvellir National Park

*Unesco World Heritage Site Þingvellir National Park (40km northeast of central Reykjavík) is Iceland's most important historical spot. Viking settlers established the world's first democratic parliament, the Alþingi, here in 930 CE. Meetings were conducted outdoors in an immense, fissured rift valley, with rivers and waterfalls all around.*

◎ MAP P100, B1

www.thingvellir.is

Rte 36/Þingvallavegur

parking 300-500kr

# Tectonic Plates

Þingvellir sits on a tectonic plate boundary where North America and Europe are tearing away from each other at 1mm to 18mm per year. The plain is scarred by dramatic fissures, ponds and rivers, including the great rift **Almannagjá**. A path skirts the fault between the clifftop visitors centre and the Alþingi site. The **Öxarárfoss** falls are on the cliffs' northern edge.

# Historic Buildings

The farmhouse in the rift, **Þingvallabær** (accessible via Rte 363; parking 300kr), was built for the 1000th anniversary of the Alþingi in 1930 by state architect Guðjón Samúelsson. It's now used as the park warden's office and prime minister's summer house. **Þingvallakirkja** (📞 482 2660; parking 300kr; ⏰9am-5pm Jun-Aug) was one of Iceland's first churches. The original was consecrated in the 11th century; the current building dates from 1859.

# Encampment Ruins

Straddling the Öxará river are ruins of temporary camps called *búðir* (booths). These stone foundations were covered during sessions and acted like stalls at modern festivals: selling food and beer. Most date to the 17th and 18th centuries; the largest, and one of the oldest, is **Biskupabúð**, north of the church.

# Alþingi

Near the dramatic Almannagjá fault and fronted by a boardwalk is the **Lögberg** (Law Rock; accessible via Rte 36 and Rte 362), where the Alþingi convened annually, and the *lögsögumaður* (law speaker) recited existing laws. After Iceland's conversion to Christianity the site shifted to the foot of the Almannagjá cliffs; that site is marked by the Icelandic flag.

---

## ★ Top Tips

○ **Þingvellir Information Centre** (Leirar Þjónustumiðstöð; ⏰9am-10pm May-Aug, to 6pm Sep-Apr) is on Rte 36 on the north side of the massive Þingvallavatn lake.

○ **Þingvellir Visitor Centre** (Gestastofa; 📞482 3613; off Rte 36; ⏰9am-7pm Jun-Aug, to 6.30pm Sep-May) is in the south.

○ Þingvellir is pronounced *thing*-vet-lir.

○ There is a nominal parking fee, but no fee to enter the site.

## ✕ Take a Break

There's a basic **cafeteria** (grilled sandwiches from 400kr; ⏰9am-10pm Apr-Oct, shorter hours Nov-Mar) in the information centre.

**Silfra Restaurant** (📞482 3415; www.ioniceland.is; Ion Luxury Adventure Hotel, Nesjavellir vid Þingvallavatn; mains lunch 2600-4500kr; ⏰11.30am-10pm), on the southern side of Þingvallavatn, features slow-food ingredients.

## Top Experience 📷
# Marvel at the Original Geysir

*One of Iceland's most famous tourist attractions, Geysir (gay-zeer; literally 'gusher') is the original hot-water spout after which all other geysers are named. Set in the beautiful Haukadalur geothermal region, the Great Geysir has been active for perhaps 800 years, and once gushed water up to 80m into the air. Now relatively dormant, its neighbour Strokkur steals the show with steady eruptions.*

◎ MAP P100, E1

Biskupstungnabraut

admission free

# Geysir & Strokkur

Geysir has gone through periods of less activity since around 1916. Earthquakes can stimulate activity, though nowadays eruptions are rare. Luckily for visitors, the reliable Strokkur sits alongside; you'll rarely wait more than 10 minutes for it to shoot an impressive 15m to 30m plume before vanishing down its enormous hole.

# Geysir Center

The large **Geysir Center** (🖉519 6020; www.geysircenter.com; Biskupstungnabraut; ⏱9am-10pm Jun-Aug, to 6pm Sep-May; 🛜👶) corrals the masses across the street from the geysers. Here you'll find a souvenir shop of mall-like proportions, an N1 petrol station and a good range of eateries.

# Surrounding Activities

Enjoy Geysir's picturesque setting by hiking in nearby Haukadalur forest, hitting the links at **Geysir Golf Course** (Haukadalsvöllur; 🖉893 8733; www.geysirgolf.is; Haukadalur 3; 9 holes Mon-Fri 2000kr, Sat & Sun 2500kr, 18 holes Mon-Fri 2500kr, Sat & Sun 3200kr, club rental 1500kr) or going salmon fishing on the Tungufljót river. On cold, clear winter evenings, look out for the Northern Lights. Many tours from Reykjavík offer these activities and more.

# Adventure Tours

Head 4km east of Geysir to Kjóastaðir horse farm, where **Geysir Hestar** (🖉847 1046; www.geysirhestar.com; Kjóastaðir 2; 1/2/3hr rides 10,000/15,000/18,000kr) offers horse riding in the area or along Hvítá River Canyon to Gullfoss.

★ **Top Tips**

○ Stand downwind only if you want a shower.

○ The undulating, hissing geothermal area containing Strokkur and Geysir was free to enter at the time of writing, though there is discussion of instituting a fee.

○ You can grab arresting photos from up the valley, looking back at the volcanic hills and erupting geyser.

✕ **Take a Break**

The Geysir Center houses a massive restaurant (mains 2700kr to 5600kr), a cafe (mains 1600kr to 3200kr) and a fast-food soup outlet (mains from 990kr).

Across the street, the restaurant at **Hótel Geysir** (🖉480 6800; www.hotelgeysir.is; Biskupstungnabraut) bustles with tour groups tucking into a daily buffet (4200kr) from noon until late.

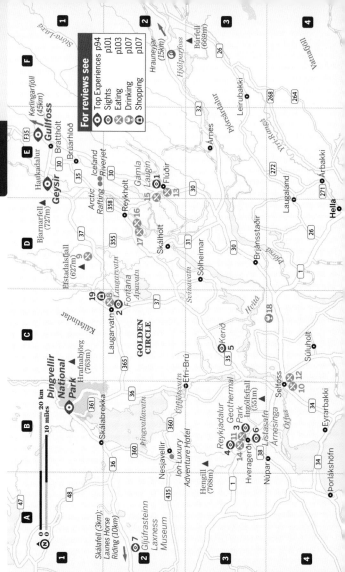

Southwest Iceland

**For reviews see**
- Top Experiences p94
- Sights p101
- Eating p103
- Drinking p107
- Shopping p107

GOLDEN CIRCLE

Þingvellir National Park

Barfell (669m)
Hrauneyjar (15km)
Hjálpurfoss

Kerlingarfjöll (45km)
Gullfoss

Geysir
Haukadalur
Bratthólt
Brúarhlöð

Bjarnarfell (727m)

Elstadalsfjall (627m)

Iceland Riverjet
Arctic Rafting

Reykholt
Gamla Laugin
Laugin
Flúðir

Skálholt

Sólheimar

Laugarvatn
Fontana
Apavatn

Kálfstindir

Hrafnabjörg (763m)

Skálabrekka

Nesjavellir

Ion Luxury Adventure Hotel

Hengill (768m)

Reykjadalur
Geothermal Park

Hveragerði
Ingólfsfjall (551m)
Listasafn
Árnesinga
Núpar
Ölfus

Kerið

Selfoss
Súluholt

Efri-Brú

Þingvallavatn
Úlfljótsvatn

Arnes
Fljótsdalur
Leirubakki

Laugaland
Árbakki
Hella

Brjánsstaðir

Þjórsá

Yamandalur
Hólaborg

Skútsafn

Gljúfrasteinn
Laxness Museum
Skálafell (3km); Laxnes Horse Riding (10km)

Eyrarbakki
Þorlákshöfn

Skála-Land

20 km
10 miles

# Sights

### Gamla Laugin GEOTHERMAL POOL

1  MAP P100, E2

Soak in this broad, calm geothermal pool, mist rising and ringed by natural rocks. The walk-ing trail along the edge of this lovely hot spring passes the local river and a series of sizzling vents and geysers. Surrounding meadows fill with wildflowers in summer. Increasingly popular, the lagoon gets packed with tour-bus crowds in mid-afternoon, so come earlier or later. (Secret Lagoon; ☑555 3351; www.secretlagoon.is; Hvammsvegur; adult/child 2800kr/free; ☺10am-10pm May-Sep, noon-8pm Oct-Apr)

### Fontana GEOTHERMAL POOL

2  MAP P100, C2

This swanky lakeside soaking spot boasts three modern wading pools and a cedar-lined steam room that's fed by a naturally occurring vent below. The cool cafe (buffet lunch/dinner 2900/3900kr) has lake views. You can rent towels or swimsuits (800kr each) and dressing gowns (1500kr) if you left yours at home. (☑486 1400; www.fontana.is; Hverabraut 1; adult/child 3800/2000kr; ☺10am-11pm early Jun-late Aug, 11am-10pm late Aug-early Jun)

### Geothermal Park GEOTHERMAL POOL

3  MAP P100, B3

The geothermal park Hverasvæðið has mud pots and steaming pools where visitors can dip their feet (but no more). Groups of 15 or more can book ahead for a guided walk (850kr per person) to learn about the area's unique geology and greenhouse power. There's also a small cafe serving tea, coffee and geothermally baked bread.

## Planning Your Journey 🔟

o Seeing the Golden Circle with your own vehicle enables you to visit at your leisure and explore attractions further afield.

o Visiting with a tour takes out the guesswork. Almost every tour company in Reykjavík offers a Golden Circle excursion.

o If you want to spend the night in the relatively small region, Laugarvatn has good services. Otherwise, camp at Þingvellir, luxe it at **Ion Luxury Adventure Hotel** (Map p100, B2; ☑482 3415; www.ioniceland.is; Nesjavellir 801; d from 44,000kr; **P @ ⸉ ≋**) or choose from accommodation along Rte 35.

o To go on to West Iceland afterwards, complete the Circle backwards, finishing with Þingvellir.

## Completing the Loop

If you're completing the Golden Circle in the traditional direction, starting at Þingvellir, then the route from Gullfoss back to the Ring Road (Rte 1) at Selfoss and the geothermal fields at Hveragerði will be the final stage of your trip. Along the way you'll find plenty to lure you to stop. Most people follow surfaced Rte 35, which passes through **Reykholt**, known for its river rafting. You can also detour slightly to **Flúðir**, with its geothermal greenhouses and hot spring, and **Skálholt**, once Iceland's religious powerhouse.

(Hveragarðurinn; ☎ 483 4601, 483 5062; Hverarmörk 13, Hveragerði; adult/child 300kr/free; �9am-6pm Mon-Sat, 10am-6pm Sun Jun-Aug, shorter hours Apr, May & Sep, closed Oct-Mar)

### Reykjadalur
GEOTHERMAL POOL

4 ◉ MAP P100, B3

Reykjadalur is a delightful geothermal valley where there's a hot river you can bathe in; bring your swimsuit. There are maps at the tourist information office to find the trail; from the trailhead car park it's a 3km hike through fields of sulphur-belching plains (it takes roughly one hour one way). Stick to marked paths, lest you melt your shoes, and leave no rubbish. (Hot River Valley; Breiðamörk)

### Kerið
VOLCANO

5 ◉ MAP P100, C3

Around 15.5km north of Selfoss on Rte 35, Kerið is a 6500-year-old explosion crater with vivid red and sienna earth and containing an ethereal green lake. Björk once performed a concert from a floating raft in the middle. Visitors can easily walk around the entire rim (it takes between 10 and 20 minutes), and go down to the lake in the crater. (Biskupstungnabraut; adult/child 400kr/free; ☯8.30am-9pm Jun-Aug, daylight hours Sep-May)

### Listasafn Árnesinga
GALLERY

6 ◉ MAP P100, B3

This airy modern-art gallery puts on superb exhibitions. When it's quiet the staff are more than happy to walk guests around the gallery, offering an insight into the art. It also has a fine cafe serving hot drinks and cakes. (☎ 483 1727; www.listasafnarnesinga.is; Austurmörk 21, Hveragerði; admission free; ☯noon-6pm daily May-Sep, Thu-Sun Oct-Apr)

### Gljúfrasteinn Laxness Museum
MUSEUM

7 ◉ MAP P100, A2

Nobel Prize–winning author Halldór Laxness (1902–98) lived in Mosfellsbær all his life. His riverside home is now the Gljúfrasteinn Laxness Museum, which is easy to access from the Reykjavík to Þingvellir road (Rte 36). The author built this classy, 1950s-style house, and it remains intact with original furniture, writing room and Laxness' fine-art collection (needlework is by his wife Auður). An audio tour leads you around. Look for his beloved Jaguar parked out the front. (☎586 8066; www.gljufrasteinn.is; Þingvallavegur, Mosfellsbær; adult/child 900kr/free; ⏰9am-5pm daily Jun-Aug, 10am-4pm Tue-Sun Sep-May)

## Eating

### Lindin ICELANDIC €€

8 MAP P100, C2

Owned by Baldur, an affable, celebrated chef, Lindin could be the best restaurant for miles. In a sweet little silver house, with simple decor and wooden tables, the restaurant faces the lake and is purely gourmet, with high-concept Icelandic fare featuring local or wild-caught ingredients. Order everything from soup to an amazing reindeer burger. Book ahead for dinner in high season. (☎486 1262; www.laugarvatn.is; Lindarbraut 2, Laugarvatn; mains 2200-5600kr; ⏰noon-10pm May-Sep, shorter hours Oct-Apr; P 📶)

### Efstidalur II ICELANDIC €€

9 MAP P100, D1

Located 12km northeast of Laugarvatn on a working dairy farm with brilliant views of hulking Hekla, Efstidalur offers tasty farm-fresh meals and amazing ice cream. The restaurant serves

Kerið

FRANCESCO TERRACCIANO/SHUTTERSTOCK ©

## Water Activities

The Golden Circle delivers a wealth of water-based adventure sports.

**Scuba Iceland** (🕿 562 7000; www.scuba.is; 2 dives from 35,000kr, snorkelling from 13,900kr) Offers dives in the Silfra fissure at Þingvellir.

**Dive.is** (🕿 578 6200; www.dive.is; Hólmaslóð 2; 2 dives at Þingvellir 34,000kr) Leads snorkelling in the glacial waters filling the fissure between Þingvellir's tectonic plates.

**Arctic Rafting** (Map p100, E1; 🕿 562 7000; www.arcticrafting.com; Drumboddsstaðir; per person rafting from 19,000kr, rafting & horse riding from 30,000kr, rafting & ATV tours from 34,000kr; ⏱ mid-May–mid-Sep) Offers a wide range of Hvítá river-rafting and combination tours.

**Iceland Riverjet** (Map p100, E1; 🕿 562 7000; www.icelandriverjet.com; Drumboddsstaðir; per person speed-boat trips 14,900kr, Golden Circle & speed-boat trips 20,000kr; ⏱ mid-Apr–Sep) Runs 40-minute jet-boat rides along the Hvítá. Offers pick-up and Golden Circle combo tours.

beef (ribeye steak) from the fields and trout (fillet served with baked veggies) from the lake. The fun ice-cream bar has windows looking into the dairy barn. (🕿 486 1186; www.efstidalur.is; Efstidalur 2; ice cream per scoop 500kr, mains 2250-5800kr; ⏱ ice-cream bar 10am-10pm, restaurant 11.30am-10pm; 🅿 🤶)

### Tryggvaskáli ICELANDIC €€

10 🍴 MAP P100, B4

Situated in Selfoss' first house (built for bridge workers in 1890), Tryggvaskáli has been lovingly renovated with antiques. Some tables in the intimate dining rooms have riverfront views and a romantic feel. The fine-dining Icelandic menu made with local produce includes dishes like

slow-cooked pork belly and plums, and mushroom-crusted cod and chorizo. The owners also operate Kaffi Krús. (🕿 482 1390; www.tryg gvaskali.is; Austurvegur 1; mains 3450-6250kr; ⏱ 11.30am-10pm Sun-Thu, to 11pm Fri & Sat)

### Varmá ICELANDIC €€€

11 🍴 MAP P100, B3

At the Frost & Fire Hotel, this wonderfully scenic restaurant boasts floor-to-ceiling windows looking over the stream and gorge. Icelandic dishes are made using fresh, local ingredients and herbs, and often with geothermal cooking techniques. The four-course wild-game menu has hot smoked goose breast with brie and reindeer steak. Book ahead in summer.

( 483 4959; www.frostogfuni.is;
Hverhamar, off Rte 376, Hveragerði;
mains 3800-7650kr, wild-game menu
10,500kr;  6-9pm;  P )

## Kaffi Krús INTERNATIONAL €€

12 🍴 MAP P100, C4

The 'Coffee Jar' is a popular cafe
and restaurant in a charming and
cosy old orange house along the
main road. There's great outdoor
space and a large selection of
Icelandic and international dishes,
from salads and pastas to fish and
farmers-market dishes. The pizza
(try the duck or langoustine) and
burgers are excellent too. ( 482
1266; www.kaffikrus.is; Austurvegur
7, Selfoss; mains 1200-4900kr;
 10am-10pm Jun-Aug, shorter hours
Sep-May)

## Minilik Ethiopian
## Restaurant ETHIOPIAN €€

13 🍴 MAP P100, E2

In the most unlikely location, Azeb
cooks up traditional Ethiopian
specialities in a welcoming,
unpretentious setting decorated
with African farming tools and
colourful linens. There are vegetarian options, plus dishes such
as awaze tibs (spicy lamb with
onion, garlic and ginger) or doro
kitfo (chicken). This is the only
Ethiopian restaurant in Iceland,
and it beckons all lovers of spice.
( 846 9798; www.minilik.is; Skeiða-
og Hrunamannavegur, Rte 30, Flúðir;
mains 2000-2500kr;  6-9pm Tue-
Fri, 2-9pm Sat & Sun; )

## Skyrgerðin CAFE €€

14 🍴 MAP P100, B3

This chilled-out cafe-cum-
restaurant incorporates rough
wood furniture, antiques and
vintage photos. Creative meals
are crafted from fresh Icelandic
ingredients and include fresh skyr
(Icelandic yoghurt) smoothies
and drinks, sliders, lasagne and
fish, plus grand cakes that are
just too tempting to resist. The
building also contains the oldest
skyr factory, hence its name.

Parties of more than 10 can
book 25- to 60-minute tours
(from 1950kr per person), in
which they'll learn how to make
skyr and taste it. Upstairs, there's
also a theatre for rent and pretty
little guest rooms (doubles with
shared bathrooms from 17,700kr).
( 481 1010; www.skyrgerdin.is;
Breiðamörk 25, Hveragerði; mains
2000-2500kr;  11am-10pm Mon-Thu,
to 11pm Fri-Sun; )

## Flúðasveppir
## Farmers Bistro ICELANDIC €€

15 🍴 MAP P100, E2

This restaurant is attached to
Iceland's only mushroom farm.
The mushroom soup is made
with a secret recipe and served
from a buffet with homemade
bread and a selection of álegg, the
Icelandic word for 'things that go
on bread', all sourced from local
greenhouses and dairy farms.
Chicken salads, lamb wraps and
vegetable patties are also on offer.

## Iceland's Ghosts, Trolls & Hidden People

When you see the vast lava fields, eerie natural formations and isolated farms that characterise much of the landscape, it comes as little surprise that many Icelanders' beliefs go beyond the scientific. It's easy to envision hidden people (*huldufólk*), ghosts and trolls roaming the hills and shores.

### Hidden People

In the lava are *jarðvergar* (gnomes), *álfar* (elves), *ljósálfar* (fairies), *dvergar* (dwarves), *ljúflingar* (lovelings), *tívar* (mountain spirits) and *englar* (angels). Stories about them have been handed down through generations, and many modern Icelanders claim to have seen the *huldufólk* or at least to know someone who has.

Stories abound about projects going wrong when workers try to build roads through *huldufólk* homes: the weather turns bad, machinery breaks down, labourers fall ill. In mid-2014 Iceland's 'whimsy factor' again made international news when a road project to link the Álftanes peninsula to the Reykjavík suburb of Garðabær was halted when campaigners warned it would disturb elf habitat.

### Ghosts & Trolls

As for Icelandic ghosts, they're substantial beings, not the wafting shadows found elsewhere. Írafell-Móri (*móri* and *skotta* are used for male and female ghosts, respectively) needed to eat supper every night, and one of the country's most famous spooks, Sel-Móri, got seasick when he stowed away in a boat. Rock stacks and certain lava formations are often said to be trolls, caught out at sunrise and turned forever to stone.

### Finding Out More

Surveys suggest that more than half of Icelanders at least entertain the possibility of the existence of *huldufólk*. But a word of warning: many Icelanders get sick of visitors asking, and they don't enjoy the 'Those cute Icelanders! They believe in pixies!' attitude. Even if they don't entirely disbelieve, they're unlikely to admit it to a stranger.

To ask all the questions you want, join a **tour** (☎694 2785; www. alfar.is; per person 4500kr; ⊙2.30pm Tue & Fri Jun–Aug) in Hafnarfjörður, 10km south of Reykjavík, or take a course at the **Icelandic Elf School** (Álfaskólinn; www.elfmuseum.com) in Reykjavík. Yes, there really is such a place, and it runs four-hour introductory classes most Fridays.

(📞519 0808; www.farmersbistro.
is; Garðastígur, Flúðir; mains from
1900kr; ⏱noon-6pm Jun-Aug, to 4pm
Sep-May)

### Friðheimar                   CAFE €€

16 ❌ MAP P100, D2

This farm is a surreal sight:
huge, bright greenhouses grow
tomatoes and a range of other
crops throughout the year using
geothermal energy. Staff sell the
produce and offer a good buffet
lunch of tomato soup, cucumber
salsa and fresh bread. It also has
reservation-only greenhouse
tours for groups of 10 or more,
and reservation-only horse shows
for groups of 15 or more. (📞486
8894; www.fridheimar.is; Friðheimar,
off Rte 35, Reykholt; dishes from
2200kr; ⏱noon-6pm)

### Café Mika        INTERNATIONAL €€

17 ❌ MAP P100, D2

Café Mika is popular with locals
for its sizeable menu, outdoor
pizza oven, sandwiches and
Icelandic mains. The roasted
langoustines (lobster) with garlic
butter is recommended. For an
extra treat, try the homemade

chocolates. (📞486 1110; https://
mika.is; Skólabraut 4, Reykholt; mains
1950-7000kr; ⏱11.30am-9pm; 📶)

## Drinking

### Ölvisholt
### Brugghús          MICROBREWERY

18 🍺 MAP P100, C4

Solid range of microbrews from
South Iceland, including the
eye-catching Lava beer. Tours
last 30 to 40 minutes (per person
3000kr) and include details about
the history of the brewery, the
brewing process, and a chance to
sample some beers. Visitors must
be 20 years or older. (📞767 5000;
www.olvisholt.is; Ölvisholti, off Rte 1;
⏱groups only by appointment)

## Shopping

### Gallerí
### Laugarvatn         ARTS & CRAFTS

19 🔒 MAP P100, C1

Local handicrafts, from Icelandic
sweets and ironwork to ceramics
and woollens. (📞486 1016; www.gal
lerilaugarvatn.is; Háholt 1, Laugarvatn;
⏱8am-6pm Thu-Tue)

# Explore ◈
# South Coast

*The Ring Road (Rte 1) sweeps southeast of Reykjavík through wide coastal plains before the landscape grows wonderfully jagged near Skógar and Vík. Inland, mountains thrust upwards and volcanoes are wreathed by mist (such as Eyjafjallajökull, which erupted in 2010, disrupting much of Europe). Here awesome glaciers glimmer as rivers carve their way to black-sand beaches and the sea.*

*The South Coast is enormous, so pick your focus. Take the Ring Road east, stopping near Hella for horse riding (p119) and Hvolsvöllur's LAVA Centre (p114) for volcano studies. Next come the grand Seljalandsfoss and Gljúfurárbui (p113) waterfalls. Other options include exploring fishing villages at Stokkseyri and Eyrarbakki, or visiting Vestmannaeyjar (p114). After lunch at Gamla Fjósið (p115) discover folk culture at Skógar (p114) and massive ice tongues at Sólheimajökull (p113). Zip along to Vík's magnificent coastline at Dyrhólaey (p112) and Reynisfjara (p112). Book ahead for dinner at Suður-Vík (p115) before powering back to Reykjavík.*

## Getting There & Around

Almost all Reykjavík-based tour companies head to the south; many local operators also pick up in Reykjavík.

🚗 Gives the most freedom; roads are good except deep inland.

🚌 This region has some of the country's most popular routes, with Strætó, Sterna and Reykjavík Excursions offering lines. In the summer Trex serves Þórsmörk and Landmannalaugar.

**South Coast Map on p110**

Eyjafjallajökull (p116) BRIAN MAUDSLEY/SHUTTERSTOCK ©

**A** **B** **C** **D**

Kerlingarfjöll
(45km)

**1** Geysir
Gullfoss

35 Brúarhlöð

Háifoss

358

30

Þórisvatn

F26

Sultartangalón

Látlisjór

Veiðivötn

**2** Flúðir
Hjálparfoss

30

Árnes

Þjórsárdalur

Búrfell
(669m)

32 26

F225

F208

4WD
only

Landmannalaugar Jökuldalur

26 Leirubakki

F208

Gjátindu

272

Ytri-Rangá

268

Hekla
(1491m)

Laufafell

Torfajökull

Kirkjufell

Eldgjá

F208

**3** Árbakki

271

Hella

264

264

Vatnafjöll

Álftavatn

F210 Fljótsdalur Tindfjallajökull

Tindfjall

F210

Hólmsá

**8** LAVA Centre
Hvolsvöllur

Eyrarbakki &
Stokkseyri
(45km)

Hlíðarendi

261

Tindfjöll
(1251m)

Þórsmörk

F261

**10**

**4**

255

Stóra-
Mörk III

Valahnúkur
(282m)

Mýrdalsjökull

Bergþórshvoll

253

Seljalandsfoss
& Gljúfurárbúi

Fimmvörðuháls

Icelandic
Mountain
Guides

Katla
(1250m)

Hafursey
(582m)

Bakki

247

Ásólfsskáli

Eyjafjallajökull

Skógafoss

**9**

**2** **7**

Skógar

**5**
Sólheimajökull

221

Mælifell
(642m)

Hjörleifshöfði
(221m)

Skógar
Folk Museum

219

Brekkur

12

**5** Heimaey
Eldfell

**6**

Vestmannaeyjar

Reynisfjara

Dyrhólaey

13 Vík

**3** **1** **11**

**6**

**A** **B** **C** **D**

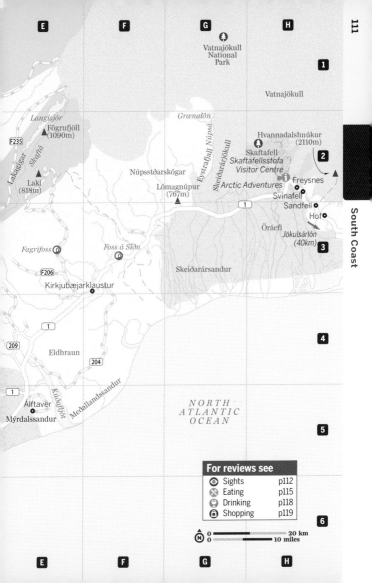

**E**   **F**   **G**   **H**

�️ Vatnajökull National Park

Vatnajökull

*Langisjór*

▲ Fögrufjöll (1090m)

F235

*Skaftá*

*Lakagígar*

▲ Laki (818m)

*Grænalón*

Núpsstaðarskógar

*Eystrafjall* *Núpsá*

*Skeiðarárjökull*

Lómagnúpur (767m)

Hvannadalshnúkur (2110m)

�️ Skaftafell
*Skaftafellsstofa Visitor Centre*
Arctic Adventures

ℹ️ Freysnes ○

Svínafell ○

Sandfell ○

1

Hof ○

Öræfi  *Jökulsárlón (40km)*

Skeiðarársandur

*Fagrifoss* 🔘

*Foss á Síðu* 🔘

F206

Kirkjubæjarklaustur ○

209

1

Eldhraun

204

*Kúðafljót*

*Meðallandssandur*

1

Álftaver ○
Mýrdalssandur

*NORTH ATLANTIC OCEAN*

**South Coast**

1

2

3

4

5

6

### For reviews see
| | | |
|---|---|---|
| 🔵 Sights | p112 |
| ❌ Eating | p115 |
| 🍸 Drinking | p118 |
| 🔒 Shopping | p119 |

Ⓝ 0 —————— 20 km
0 —————— 10 miles

**E**   **F**   **G**   **H**

# Sights

## Reynisfjara BEACH

1 ◉ MAP P110, C5

On the western side of Reynisfjall, the high ridge above Vík, Rte 215 leads 5km down to the black-sand beach Reynisfjara. It's backed by an incredible stack of **basalt columns** that look like a magical church organ, and there are outstanding views west to Dyrhólaey. Surrounding cliffs are pocked with caves formed from twisted basalt, and puffins belly-flop into the crashing sea during summer.

Immediately offshore are the towering **Reynisdrangur** sea stacks. At all times watch for rogue waves: people are regularly swept away. (Rte 215)

## Skógafoss WATERFALL

2 ◉ MAP P110, B5

This 62m-high waterfall topples over a rocky cliff at the western edge of Skógar in dramatic style. Climb the steep staircase alongside for giddy views, or walk to the foot of the falls, shrouded in sheets of mist and rainbows. Legend has it that a settler named Þrasi hid a chest of gold behind Skógafoss. The top of the waterfall is the start of the dramatic Fimmvörðuháls trek, which continues 23km on to Þórsmörk, the land of the gods. (Skogafossvegur, off Rte 1)

## Dyrhólaey WILDLIFE RESERVE

3 ◉ MAP P110, C5

One of the South Coast's most recognisable natural formations is the rocky plateau and huge

---

### Skaftafell & Vatnajökull National Park

Massive **Vatnajökull National Park** (Map p110, G1; www.vjp.is) absorbs nearly 14% of the entire country. Skaftafell, the jewel in the park's crown, encompasses a breathtaking collection of peaks and glaciers. Here thundering waterfalls, twisted birch woods and tangled rivers border the brilliant blue-white Vatnajökull with its enormous ice tongues, many of which are visible from the Ring Road in the southeast.

**Skaftafellsstofa visitor centre** (Map p110, H2; ☏ 470 8300; ◷ 8am-7pm Jun-Sep, 9am-6pm Feb-May & Oct, 10am-6pm Nov-Jan; 🛜) has exhibitions and a summer-time cafe, and information on walks, such as the 1.8km one to **Svartifoss** (Black Falls), a moody waterfall flanked by geometric black basalt columns. **Arctic Adventures** (Glacier Guides; Map p110, H2; ☏ 562 7000; www.glacierguides.is) leads glacier walks and adventure tours.

CHRISTOPHER CZERMAK/SHUTTERSTOCK ©

Reynisfjara

stone sea arch at Dyrhólaey (*deer-lay*), which rises dramatically from the surrounding plain 10km west of Vík, at the end of Rte 218. Visit its crashing black-sand beaches and get awesome views from atop the promontory. The islet is a nature reserve that's rich in bird life, including puffins; some or all of it can be closed during nesting season (15 May to 25 June). (Rte 218)

### Seljalandsfoss & Gljúfurárbui WATERFALL

4 ⊙ MAP P110, A4

From the Ring Road you'll see the beautiful high falls at Seljalandsfoss, which tumble over a rocky scarp into a deep, green pool. A (slippery) path runs around the back of the waterfall. A few hundred metres further down the Þórsmörk road, Gljúfurárbui gushes into a hidden canyon. (Off Rte 249, near Rte 1; parking 700kr)

### Sólheimajökull GLACIER

5 ⊙ MAP P110, C5

One of the easiest glacial tongues to reach is Sólheimajökull. This icy outlet glacier unfurls from the main Mýrdalsjökull ice cap and is a favourite spot for glacial walks and ice climbing. Rte 221 leads 4.2km off the Ring Road to a small car park and the **Arcanum base camp** (☏ 487 1500; www.arcanum.is; Rte 221; glacier walks from 9500kr, ATV tours from 19,000kr, snowmobile rides per 2 people from 27,000kr; ☉ 9.30am-5pm) office, from where you can walk the 800m to the ice along a wide track edging the glacial lagoon. Don't attempt to climb onto the glacier unguided.

## Eldfell

VOLCANO

6 ⊙ MAP P110, A5

The 221m-high volcanic cone Eldfell appeared from nowhere in the early hours of 23 January 1973. Once the fireworks finished, heat from the volcano provided Heimaey with geothermal energy from 1976 to 1985. Today the ground is still hot enough in places to bake bread or char wood. Eldfell is an easy climb from town, up the collapsed northern wall of the crater; stick to the path, as the islanders are trying to save their latest volcano from erosion. (Off Fellavegur; P)

## Skógar Folk Museum

MUSEUM

7 ⊙ MAP P110, C5

The highlight of little Skógar is the wonderful Skógar Folk Museum, which covers all aspects of Icelandic life. The vast collection was put together by Þórður Tómasson over roughly 75 years – he retired as the museum's curator at the age of 92. There are also restored buildings – a church, a turf-roofed farmhouse, cowsheds – and a huge, modern building that houses an interesting transport and communication museum, a basic cafe and a shop. (Skógasafn; ☑487 8845; www.skogasafn.is; Skógavegur, near Rte 1; adult/child 2000kr/free; ⊙9am-6pm Jun-Aug, 10am-5pm Sep-May)

## Vestmannaeyjar

Vestmannaeyjar (Westman Islands; Map p110, A5) form 15 eye-catching silhouettes off the shore. Heimaey is the only inhabited island, and its town lies between escarpments and volcanoes (part of a 1973 eruption that almost covered the village). Heimaey is famous for its 10 million puffins, the **Þjóðhátíð festival** (National Festival Þjóðhátíð Vestmannaeyjar; www.dalurinn.is; Dalvegur; tickets 23,900kr, ferry trip 1380kr; ⊙Jul or Aug) and its excellent eruption museum, **Eldheimar** (Pompeii of the North; ☑488 2700; www.eldheimar.is; Gerðisbraut 10; adult/child 2300/1200kr; ⊙11am-6pm).

It's a great day trip on the Herjólfur ferry. **Slippurinn** (☑481 1515; www.slippurinn.com; Strandvegur 76; lunch 2400-7200kr, dinner mains 3700-4900kr, set menu 6400-9900kr; ⊙noon-2.30pm & 5-10pm early May–mid-Sep; 🛜) serves superb meals.

## Fishing Village Life

South of the Ring Road the tiny fishing villages of Stokkseyri and Eyrarbakki are refreshingly local-feeling. Stokkseyri has a quirky **Elves Museum** (☑ 483 1202; www.icelandicwonders.com; Hafnargata; adult/child 1500/1200kr; ☉ 1-6pm Jun-Aug) and **Draugasetrið** (Ghost Museum; ☑ 854 4510; http://icelandicwonders.is; Hafnargata 9, off Rte 33; adult/child 2000/1200kr; ☉ 1-6pm Jun-Aug), a haunted house run by a gaggle of bloodthirsty teens.

Eyrarbakki's **Flói Nature Reserve** (☑ 562 0477; www.fuglavernd.is; off Rte 34) is super for birdwatching, and **Húsið á Eyrarbakka** (House at Eyrarbakki; ☑ 483 1504; www.husid.com; Eyrargata; adult/child incl Sjóminjasafnið á Eyrarbakka 1000kr/free; ☉ 11am-6pm mid-May–mid-Sep) is one of Iceland's oldest homes.

Come supper time, duelling restaurants **Við Fjöruborðið** (☑ 483 1550; www.fjorubordid.is; Eyrarbraut 3a, Stokkseyri; mains 2900-7900kr; ☉ noon-9pm; [P] ☎) and **Rauða Húsið** (☑ 483 3330; www.raudahusid.is; Búðarstígur 4, Eyrarbakki; mains 2700-5800kr; ☉ noon-9pm; ☎) contend for the 'best lobster bisque' award.

## LAVA Centre
MUSEUM

8 ◉ MAP P110, A4

Essentially displaying Iceland's birth story, the LAVA Centre is a full-blown multimedia experience on volcanic and seismic life. Divided into multiple chambers, the museum includes an earthquake simulator (equivalent to four on the Richter scale) and a fog of smoke resembling volcanic ash. Visitors will likely leave with a sharper understanding of how earthquakes and volcanoes interconnect. (Iceland Volcano & Earthquake Centre; ☑ 415 5200; www.lavacentre.is; Austurvegur 14, Hvolsvöllur; adult/child 2400kr/free, cinema only 1200kr/free, exhibition & cinema 3200kr/free; ☉ exhibition 9am-7pm, lava house to 9pm)

# Eating

## Gamla Fjósið
ICELANDIC €€€

9 ⊗ MAP P110, B5

Built in a former cowshed that was in use until 1999, this charming eatery's focus is on farm-fresh and grass-fed meaty mains, from burgers to Volcano Soup, a spicy meat stew. The hardwood floor and low beams are balanced by polished dining tables, large wooden hutches and friendly staff. (Old Cowhouse; ☑ 487 7788; www.gamlafjosid.is; Hvassafell, off Rte 1; mains 3900-6900kr, burgers from 2070kr, Volcano Soup 2400kr; ☉ 11am-9pm Jun-Aug, shorter hours Sep-May; ☎)

# Icelandic Volcanoes

Situated on the Mid-Atlantic Ridge, a massive 18,000km-long rift between two of the earth's major tectonic plates, Iceland is a shifting, steaming lesson in classroom geology. A mere baby in geological terms, Iceland is the youngest country in Europe, formed by underwater volcanic eruptions along the joint of the North American and Eurasian plates 17 to 20 million years ago. The earth's crust in Iceland is only a third of its normal thickness, and magma (molten rock) continues to rise from deep within, forcing the two plates apart. The result is clearly visible at Þingvellir, where the great rift Almannagjá broadens by between 1mm and 18mm per year.

The thin crust and grating plates are responsible for a whole host of exciting volcanic activities, but fissure eruptions and their associated craters are probably the most common type of eruption in Iceland. The still-volatile Lakagígar crater row around **Mt Laki** is the country's most unearthly example. It produced the largest lava flow in human history in the 18th century, covering an area of 565 sq km to a depth of 12m.

## Subglacial & Submarine Eruptions

Several of Iceland's liveliest volcanoes lie beneath glaciers, which makes for drama as molten lava and ice interact. The eruption of **Eyjafjallajökull** in 2010 caused a *jökulhlaup* (flooding caused by volcanic eruption beneath an ice cap) before throwing up the famous ash plume that grounded Europe's aeroplanes. Iceland's most active volcano, **Grímsvötn**, which lies beneath Vatnajökull ice cap, behaved similarly in 2011.

In 1963 the island of **Surtsey** exploded from the sea, giving scientists the opportunity to study how smouldering chunks of newly created land are colonised by plants and animals. Surtsey is off-limits to visitors, but you can climb many classical-looking cones such as **Hekla**, once thought to be the gateway to Hell; **Eldfell**, which did its best to bury the town of Heimaey in 1973; and **Snæfellsjökull**, on the Snæfellsnes Peninsula.

The Icelandic Met Office (www.vedur.is) keeps track of eruptions and the earthquakes that tend to precede them, plus the emissions that follow.

### Suður-Vík
ICELANDIC, ASIAN €€

The friendly ambience, in a warmly lit building with hardwood floors, exposed beams and interesting artwork, helps to elevate this restaurant beyond its competition. Food is hearty, ranging from farm plates and quinoa salad with chicken to pizzas and Asian dishes (think spicy Panang curry with rice). Book ahead in summer. For a nightcap head to the **Man Cave** (beers from 1000kr; ☽6pm-late) downstairs. It's located near Smiðjan Brugghús (see 12 🍴 Map p110, D5).(☎ 487 1515; www.facebook.com/Sudurvik; Suðurvíkurvegur 1, Vík; mains 1300-5350kr; ☽noon-10pm, shorter hours in winter)

### Hafið Bláa
SEAFOOD €€

10  MAP P110, A3

Three kilometres west of Eyrarbakki on Rte 34 at the Ölfusá Bridge, this seafood restaurant sits on the water's edge in an ovoid building, with a beautiful arcing-wood interior. Even if you don't get a table overlooking the ocean, the sweeping estuary views on the opposite side are equally impressive. The menu offers a small range of seafood and lamb. (☎ 483 1000; www.hafidblaa.is; Rte 34; mains 2300-3900kr; ☽noon-9pm Jun-Aug, shorter hours Sep-May)

### Halldórskaffi
INTERNATIONAL €€

Inside Vík's Brydebúð museum, this lively, timber-lined all-rounder is very popular in high season for its crowd-pleasing menu ranging from burgers and pizza to lamb fillet. Be prepared to wait in summer since it doesn't take reservations. The cakes are too tempting to resist – the Icelandic meringue cake is particularly

Skógar Folk Museum (p114)

MAX TOPCHII/SHUTTERSTOCK ©

good. It's near Smiðjan Brugghús (see **12** Map p110, D5). (📞 487 1202; www.halldorskaffi.com; Víkurbraut 28; mains 2000-5000kr; 🕙noon-10pm Jun-Aug, to 9pm Sep-May)

### Eldstó Art Café
CAFE €€

Eldstó serves fresh-brewed coffee, homemade daily specials (such as traditional Icelandic flatbread with smoked lamb, and hot chocolate, for 1350kr) and main courses like slowly roasted lamb shank or oven-baked salmon. Burgers and salads are on the menu too, plus triple-stacked homemade cakes. There are several tables in the cosy, welcoming space. Near the LAVA Centre (see **8** 🎯 Map p110, A4) (📞 482 1011; www.eldsto.is; Austurvegur

2, Hvolsvöllur; mains 2150-4250kr; 🕙10am-10pm Jun-Aug; 🅿🛜)

### Black Beach Restaurant
CAFE €€

**11** ❌ MAP P110, D5

Black volcanic cubes, meant to mimic the nearby black-sand beach Reynisfjara with its famous basalt columns, house this contemporary cafe that serves homemade cakes and snacks during the day, plus fish and chips, soups and chicken salads. Plate-glass windows give views to the ocean and Dyrhólaey beyond. (Svarta Fjaran; 📞 571 2718; www.svartafjaran.com; Reynisfjara, Rte 215; snacks 990kr, dinner mains 2200-4000kr; 🕙11am-9pm; 🛜)

Black Beach Restaurant

GESTUR GISLASON/GETTY IMAGES ©

## Horse Riding

Many horse farms around the south, especially near Hella and Hvolsvöllur, and between Skógar and Vík, offer rides or multiday tours, and most have accommodation. Expect to pay between 8000kr and 9000kr for a one-hour ride and from 25,000kr for a day-long ride, though prices can drop for groups.

Outfitters include **Skeiðvellir** (Icelandic HorseWorld; ☎487 6572, horse riding 899 5619; www.skeidvellir.is; Rte 26, Skeiðvellir farm; stable visit adult/child 2000kr/free, 1/2hr horse rides 9500/15,000kr), **Hella Horse Rental** (☎864 5950; www.hellahorserental.is; Gaddstaðaflatir, off Rte 1; 1.5/3hr tours from 8500/15,000kr; 🖐), **Eldhestar** (☎480 4800; http://eldhestar.is/tours; Vallavegur, off Hringvegur; 1hr tour adult/child from 8000/6400kr), **Sólhestar** (☎892 3066; www.solhestar.is; Borgargerði, Ölfus, off Hvammsvegur/Rte 374; 1/2hr tours from 9000/12,000kr) and multiday specialists **Hekluhestar** (☎487 6598; www.hekluhestar.is; Austvaðsholt; multiday rides from 275,000kr).

# Drinking

## Smiðjan Brugghús MICROBREWERY

12 🍺 MAP P110, D5

Vík's hippest hangout is warehouse-style with windows looking onto the brewing room and blackboards displaying 10 craft beers on tap. Hop aficionados can try Icelandic India Pale Ales, pale ale, porter and farmhouse ale with a handful of different burgers (including a vegan patty). (http://smidjanbrugghus.is; Sunnubraut 15; ⏲11.30am-midnight Sun-Thu, to 1am Fri & Sat)

# Shopping

## Una Local Products ARTS & CRAFTS

This large hangar on the Ring Road near the LAVA Centre (see 8 ⊙ Map p110, A4) is loaded with all manner of handmade Icelandic crafts, from fish-skin purses to woolly sweaters, jewellery and leather goods. (Sveitabúðin Una; ☎544 5455; www.unalocalstore.is; Austurvegur 4, Hvolsvöllur; ⏲10am-6pm; 📶)

## Icewear GIFTS & SOUVENIRS

13 🎁 MAP P110, D5

The big Icewear souvenir and knitwear shop next to the N1 petrol station is a coach-tour hit. You can peek inside the factory portion to see woollen wear being made and there are Icelandic souvenirs by the bucketload, plus the Ice Cave Restaurant. (☎487 1250; www.icewear.is; Austurvegur 20, Vík; ⏲8am-10pm)

## Worth a Trip 🔭
# Jökulsárlón

*One of Iceland's most magical sights, Jökulsárlón glacier lagoon is filled with spectacular, luminous-blue icebergs drifting out to sea. The hours will zip by as you go scouting for seals or take a boat trip amid wondrous ice sculptures (some striped with ash from volcanic eruptions) as they spin in the changing light. The icebergs calve from Breiðamerkurjökull glacier, an offshoot of Vatnajökull ice cap.*

### Getting There

🚗 Driving makes overnighting easy.

🚌 From Reykjavík take Sterna bus 12/12a or Strætó bus 51, year round. Reykjavík Excursions bus 15 travels between Skaftafell and Jökulsárlón in July and August.

# The Lagoon

Although it looks as though it's been here since the last ice age, the lagoon is only about 80 years old. Until the mid-1930s Breiðamerkurjökull reached the Ring Road; it's now retreating rapidly (up to a staggering 500m per year), and the lagoon is growing. Icebergs can spend up to five years floating in the 25-sq-km-plus, 260m-deep lagoon before they travel out to sea.

## Boat Tours

Forty-minute trips with **Glacier Lagoon Amphibious Boat Tours** (☏ 478 2222; www.icelagoon.is; adult/child 5700/2000kr; ⊙ 9am-7pm Jun-Sep, 10am-5pm May & Oct) trundle along the shore before driving into the water. It also offers Zodiac tours, as does **Ice Lagoon Zodiac Boat Tours** (☏ 860 9996; www.icelagoon.com; adult/child 9700/6200kr; ⊙ 9am-5.30pm May-Sep), which speed up to the glacier edge (not done by the amphibious boats) before cruising back slowly. Book ahead.

## Wildlife

Keep a lookout for seals bobbing up and down in the lagoon between the brilliant bergs. The zooming Arctic terns nest not only on the shore but also on some of the larger ice chunks.

## The River Mouth

Visit **Diamond Beach** at the Jökulsá river mouth to see ice boulders resting photogenically on the black-sand beach as part of their final journey out to sea.

---

## ★ Top Tips

○ Consider sleeping over: Jökulsárlón is 375km from Reykjavík (4½ hours one way).

○ Aim for evenings for fewer crowds.

○ Parking areas on the Ring Road west of the car park have trails to less-touristed shores.

○ Amphibious boat tours generally run May to October.

○ Restroom facilities are inadequate.

○ Nearby are glacier walks in Vatnajökull National Park (p112) and hikes on **Hvannadalshnúkur** (☏ Reykjavík 587 9999, Skaftafell 894 2959; www.mountainguides.is).

## ✕ Take a Break

A lagoon-side **cafe** (snacks 900-1200kr; ⊙ 9am-7pm Jun-Sep, to 6pm Mar-May & Oct, to 5pm Nov-Feb) has snacks. **Heimahumar** (lobster rolls 1800kr; ⊙ 11.30am-6pm May-Oct) offers hot dogs and lobster rolls. **Nailed It** (meals 1700kr; ⊙ noon-5.30pm) has delicious fish and chips.

# Explore ⊕
# Snæfellsnes Peninsula

*Sparkling fjords, dramatic volcanic peaks, sheer sea cliffs, sweeping beaches and crunchy lava flows make up the 100km-long Snæfellsnes Peninsula. The area is crowned by the glistening ice cap of Snæfellsjökull. Good roads and regular buses mean it's an easy trip from Reykjavík, offering a cross section of the best of Iceland in a compact space.*

*Begin in characterful Stykkishólmur, whale watching on Breiðafjörður (p128) or exploring the town's rich maritime past at Norska Húsið (p127). After a quick visit to the basalt island of Súgandisey (p128), lunch can be local mussels at Sjávarpakkhúsið (p130) or bakery treats at Nesbrauð (p130). Next comes photo ops at Game of Thrones location Kirkjufell (p127) before heading to Snæfellsjökull National Park (p124) and a pre-booked Vatnshellir lava cave tour (p128). Then wander black-sand Djúpalón Beach (p127), see the lighthouse at Malarrif (p127) and finish with a fine meal at Fosshotel Hellnar Restaurant (p130).*

## Getting There & Around

🚗 Hiring a car is the easiest option.

🚌 You can get between Reykjavík and the Snæfellsnes Peninsula (4140kr, 2½ hours) by changing in Borgarnes. Between mid-May and mid-September, one or two Strætó buses run daily from Borgarnes to Stykkishólmur (bus 58), and from Stykkishólmur, via Hellissandur, to Arnarstapi (bus 82). All services are reduced in winter.

### Snæfellsnes Peninsula Map on p126

Stykkishólmur (p127) JEAFISH PING/SHUTTERSTOCK ©

## Top Sights 📷

# Experience the Wonders of Snæfellsjökull National Park

*Snæfellsjökull National Park encompasses much of the western tip of Snæfellsnes Peninsula, and wraps around the rugged slopes of the glacier Snæfellsjökull, the icy fist at the end of the long Snæfellsnes arm. Around its flanks lie lava tubes, protected lava fields, which are home to native Icelandic fauna, and prime coastal bird- and whale-watching spots.*

◎ MAP P126, B3

📞 436 6860

www.snaefellsjokull.is

## Visitor Centre & Hikes

Hiking trails criss-cross the park, and the **Snæfellsjökull National Park Visitor Centre** (☎ 591 2000, 436 6888; ⏰ 10am-5pm daily late Apr-Oct, 11am-4pm Mon-Fri rest of year; 📶) in Malarrif sells maps (free online) and gives advice (as do area tourist offices). Rangers have summer programmes of free guided tours.

## Snæfellsjökull

It's easy to see why Jules Verne chose Snæfell for his adventure *Journey to the Centre of the Earth*: the peak was torn apart when the volcano beneath exploded. Today the crater is filled with the ice cap (highest point 1446m; *jökull* means 'glacier'). To reach its summit take a tour from Hellnar or Arnarstapi; some operators pick up in Reykjavík.

## Öndverðarnes

At the westernmost tip of Snæfellsnes an ancient lava flow leads to Öndverðarnes peninsula, great for **whale watching**. From the last parking area (at a squat, orange lighthouse), walk to the tip of the peninsula, or head 200m northeast to **Fálki**, an ancient stone well thought to have three waters: fresh, holy and ale! The **Svörtuloft bird cliffs** (Saxhólsbjarg) are to the south.

## Djúpalón Beach & Dritvík

On the southwest coast, the black-sand beach of Djúpalónssandur (p127) offers dramatic walks with rock formations, shipwreck debris, sea stacks and a striking rock arch. Tramp north over the craggy headland to reach black-sand **Dritvík**, once the largest Icelandic fishing station, now lonely ruins.

### ★ Top Tips

● Dress warmly and wear hiking boots and gloves to take a pre-booked, 45-minute guided tour of the fascinating Vatnshellir lava cave (p128).

● Stykkishólmur, on the peninsula's northern coast, is the region's largest town and a good base for overnighting.

● Even the well trained and outfitted are not allowed to ascend the glacier without a local guide; contact the Snæfellsjökull National Park Visitor Centre, or take a tour.

### ✕ Take a Break

Hellnar has the small, welcoming **Primus Café** (☎ 865 6740; www.facebook.com/primuskaffi; Hellnavegur; mains 1600-2600kr; ⏰ 10am-9pm May–mid-Sep, 11am-4pm mid-Sep–Apr) for simple meals.

Fjöruhúsið (p130), by the rocky waterfront, serves soups and coffee with a wonderful view over seabird nests and the shore.

Snæfellsnes Peninsula

Breiðafjörður

Flatey (18km); Brjánslækur (30km)

Stykkishólmur
Súgandisey
See Enlargement
Helgafell (73m)
Skjöldur
Drápuhlíðarfjall (527m)
Ljósufjöll
Harðarfell (722m)
Borgarnes (65km); Reykjavík (137km)

Búðardalur (50km)

Vatnaleið
Berserkjahraun
Selvallavatn
Hraunsfjarðarvatn
Kerlingarfjall (585m)
Kerlingarskarð
Móhraun
Vegamót
Stakkhamar
Baulárvallavatn
Hólsfjall

Breiðafjörður

Láki Tours
Grundarfjörður
Kirkjufell
Helgrindudir
Porgeirsfell
Snæfellsnes Peninsula
Lýsuhólslaug
Lýsuhóll
Lýsufoll
Búðir
Ytri-Tunga

Hafflörður

Faxaflói

Búlandshöfði

Ólafsvík
Rif
Burfell
Eysteinsdalur
Prðbárheðta
Mæifell
Stóri Kambur
Snæfellsjökull (1446m)
Snæfellsjökull Glacier Tours
Rauðfeldsgjá
Breiðavík
Búðahraun
Bjóaklettur (88m)
Go West!
Arnarstapi
Hellnar

Hellissandur
Skarðsvík
Neshraun
Saxhóll Crater
Klukkufoss
Snæfellsjökull National Park
Stúpafell (526m)
Dritvík
Djúpalón Beach
Malarrif

Denmark Strait

**For reviews see**
○ Top Experiences p124
○ Sights p127
○ Experiences p129
✗ Entertainment p131
🛍 Shopping p131

**Enlargement (Hellissandur):**
Skólastígur
Sæbraut
Hafnargata
Norská Húsið
Fruarstígur
Adalgata
Landsgarðsund
Sætours
Austurgata
Volcano Museum
Rif
Maðkavík

200 m
0.1 miles

10 km
5 miles

# Sights

### Djúpalón Beach
BEACH

1  MAP P126, B3

On the southwest coast, Rte 572 leads off Rte 574 to wild black-sand beach **Djúpalónssandur**. It's a dramatic place to walk, with rock formations (an elf church, and a **kerling** – a troll woman), two brackish pools (for which the beach was named) and the rock-arch **Gatklettur**. Some of the black sands are covered in pieces of rusted metal from the English trawler *Eding,* which was shipwrecked here in 1948. An asphalt car park and public toilets allow tour-bus access, and crowds.

### Malarrif
LIGHTHOUSE

2  MAP P126, B4

About 2km south of Djúpalón Beach, a paved road leads down to the rocket-shaped lighthouse at Malarrif, from where you can walk 1km east along the cliffs to the rock pillars at **Lóndrangar** (an eroded crater; it also has its own parking off Rte 574), which surge up into the air in surprising pinnacles. Locals say that elves use the lava formations as a church. A bit further to the east lie the **Þúfubjarg bird cliffs**, also accessible from Rte 574. (admission free)

### Kirkjufell
MOUNTAIN

3  MAP P126, D2

Kirkjufell (463m), guardian of Grundarfjörður's northwestern

vista, is said to be one of the most photographed spots in Iceland, appearing in *Game of Thrones* and on everyone's Instagram. Ask staff at the **Saga Centre** (Eyrbyggja Heritage Centre; 438 1881; www.grundarfjordur.is; Grundargata 35; 9am-5pm) if you want to climb it; they may be able to find you a guide. Two spots involving a rope climb make it dangerous to scale when wet or without local knowledge. Kirkjufell is backed by the roaring waterfalls of **Kirkjufellsfoss**.

### Norska Húsið
MUSEUM

4  MAP P126, A1

Stykkishólmur's quaint maritime charm comes from the cluster of wooden warehouses, shops and homes around the town's harbour. Most date back about 150 years. One of the most interesting (and oldest) is the Norska Húsið, now the regional museum. Built by trader and amateur astronomer Árni Thorlacius in 1832, the house

---

**Stykkishólmur** ⓘ

The charming town of **Stykkishólmur** (Map p126, E1; www.visitstykkisholmur.is) is built around a natural harbour tipped by a basalt islet. A laid-back attitude, a sprinkling of brightly coloured 19th-century buildings and a good range of restaurants and places to stay ensure it's an excellent base.

## Tours

**Go West!** (Map p126, C3; Arnarstapi; ☎ 695 9995; www.gowest.is) Eco-friendly cycling, hiking, hot-spring and glacier tours.

**Láki Tours** (Map p126, D2; ☎ 546 6808; www.lakitours.com; Nesvegur 5, Grundarfjörður) Puffins, whales and fishing from Grundarfjörður or Ólafsvík.

**Lýsuhóll** (Map p126, D3; ☎ 435 6716; www.lysuholl.is) Horse riding in southern Snæfellsnes. Also run by **Stóri Kambur** (Map p126, C3; ☎ 852 7028; www.storikambur.is; Rte 574; ☺ late May–mid-Sep).

**Seatours** (Sæferðir; Map p126, B1; ☎ 433 2254; www.seatours.is; Smiðjustígur 3, Stykkishólmur; ☺ 8am-8pm mid-May–mid-Sep, 9am-5pm rest of year) Boat trips, including the much-touted 'Viking Sushi'.

**Snæfellsjökull Glacier Tours** (Map p126, C3; ☎ 865 0061; www.the glacier.is; Litli-Kambur; snowcat tours adult/child 7900/5000kr; snowmobile tours 18,000kr; ☺ May-Aug) Explorations by snowcat and snowmobile.

**Summit Adventure Guides** (☎ 787 0001; www.summitguides.is) Tours of the Vatnshellir lava tube.

---

has been skilfully restored and displays a wonderfully eclectic selection of local antiquities. On the 2nd floor you visit Árni's home, an upper-class 19th-century residence. (Norwegian House; ☎ 433 8114; www.norskahusid.is; Hafnargata 5; adult/child 1000kr/free; ☺ 11am-6pm daily May-Aug. 2-5pm Tue-Thu Sep-Apr)

### Breiðafjörður  NATURAL FEATURE

**5** ◎ MAP P126, F1

Stykkishólmur's jagged peninsula pushes north into stunning Breiðafjörður, a broad waterway separating the Snæfellsnes from the looming cliffs of the distant Westfjords. According to local legend, there are only two things in the world that cannot be counted: the stars in the night sky and the craggy islets in the bay. You *can* count on epic vistas and a menagerie of wild birds (puffins, eagles, guillemots). Boat trips, including whale watching and puffin viewing, are available from Stykkishólmur, Grundarfjörður and Ólafsvík.

### Súgandisey  ISLAND

**6** ◎ MAP P126, F1

The basalt island Súgandisey features a scenic lighthouse and grand views across Breiðafjörður. Reach it via the causeway at Stykkishólmur harbour.

## Volcano Museum

MUSEUM

7  MAP P126, A1

The Volcano Museum, housed in Stykkishólmur's old cinema, is the brainchild of vulcanologist Haraldur Sigurðsson, and features art depicting volcanoes, plus a small collection of interesting lava ('magma bombs') and artefacts from eruptions. A film screens upstairs. (Eldfjallasafn; 433 8154; www.eldfjallasafn.is; Aðalgata 8; adult/child 1000kr/free; 10am-5pm daily Jun-Aug, 11am-5pm Tue-Sat Sep-May)

# Eating

## Bjargarsteinn Mathús

SEAFOOD €€

8 MAP P126, D2

This superb waterfront restaurant on the point in Grundarfjörður is operated by seasoned restaurateurs who have created a lively menu of Icelandic dishes, with an emphasis on seafood and everything fresh. Desserts are delicious too. The seasonal menu is always changing, the decor is quaint, and views to Kirkjufell are stupendous. ( 438 6770; www.facebook.com/Bjargarsteinnrestaurant; Sólvellir 15; mains 2800-4900kr; 4-10pm Jun-Aug, 5-9pm Sep–mid-Dec & mid-Jan–May; )

## Narfeyrarstofa

ICELANDIC €€

9 MAP P126, B1

This charming restaurant is the Snæfellsnes' darling fine-dining destination with an interesting history. Book a table on the 2nd floor for romantic lighting

Djúpalón Beach (p127)

PAUL TIPTON/SHUTTERSTOCK ©

and harbour views. (📞533 1119; www.narfeyrarstofa.is; Aðalgata 3, Stykkishólmur; mains 2000-5000kr; 🕙11.30am-10pm May-Sep, reduced hours Oct-Apr; 🎫)

### Fjöruhúsið
SEAFOOD €€

10 🍴 MAP P126, B3

Follow the stone path to the ocean's edge for some of the renowned fish soup at beautifully situated, Fjöruhúsið. Located at the trailhead of the scenic Hellnar–Arnarstapi path. (📞435 6844; www.facebook.com/FjoruhusidHellnum; cakes & quiches 950kr, mains 2500-2800kr; 🕙11am-10pm Jun-Aug, reduced hours Mar-May & Sep-Nov)

### Fosshotel Hellnar Restaurant
ICELANDIC €€

11 🍴 MAP P126, B3

Even if you're not overnighting at Hótel Hellnar, we highly recommend having dinner at its restaurant, which sources local organic produce for its Icelandic menu. Reserve ahead. (📞435 6820; mains 3800-5000kr; 🕙6-10pm Mar-Nov; 🅿️🛜)

### Sjávarpakkhúsið
ICELANDIC €€

12 🍴 MAP P126, A1

This old fish-packing house has been transformed into a wood-lined cafe-bar with harbourfront outdoor seating. It's a great daytime hang-out too, and on weekend evenings it turns into a popular bar where locals come to jam. (📞438 1800; www.sjavarpakkhusid.is; Hafnargata 2, Stykkishólmur; mains 2800-3500kr; 🕙noon-10pm; 🛜)

### Nesbrauð
BAKERY €

13 🍴 MAP P126, E1

On the road into Stykkishólmur, this bakery is a good choice for a quick breakfast or lunch. Stock up on sugary confections such as *kleinur* (traditional twisty doughnuts) or *ástar pungur* (literally 'love balls'; fried balls of dough and raisins). (📞438 1830; www.facebook.com/nesbraudehf; Nesvegur 1, Stykkishólmur; snacks 400-1200kr; 🕙7.30am-5pm Mon-Fri, from 8am Sat & Sun)

---

### Favourite Trails: Between Arnarstapi & Hellnar

One of the most popular (and scenic) hiking trails on Snæfellsnes Peninsula is the 2.5km coastal walk (around 40 minutes) between Hellnar and Arnarstapi. This slender trail follows the coastline through a nature reserve, passing lava flows and eroded stone caves. During tumultuous weather, waves spray through the rocky arches; when it's fine, look for nesting seabirds.

## A Climb & A Soak

A favourite Snæfellsnes hike is up roadside scoria crater **Saxhöll** (Map p126, B3; Rte 574), which was responsible for some of the lava on the western side of the peninsula. From the base it's a 300m climb for magnificent views over the Neshraun lava flows. Then head east over to **Lýsuhólslaug** (Map p126, D3; ☏ 433 9917; lysuholslaug@gmail.com; adult/child 1000/300kr; ⏲11am-8.30pm Jun–mid-Aug), where a geothermal source pumps in carbonated, mineral-filled waters at a perfect 37°C to 39°C. Don't be alarmed that the pool is a murky green: the iron-rich water attracts some serious algae.

## Hraun
INTERNATIONAL €€

14 🍴 MAP P126, B2

This upbeat establishment on Ólafsvík's main road cheerfully fills a blond-wood building with a broad front deck. The only gig in town besides fast food, it does excellent fresh mussels and lamb, burgers and fish, and has beer on tap. (☏ 431 1030; www.facebook.com/hraun.veitingahus; Grundarbraut 2, Ólafsvík; mains 2900-5900kr; ⏲11.30am-9pm Mon-Fri, noon-9pm Sat & Sun Jun-Aug, some weekends Sep-May; 🛜)

# Entertainment
## Freezer Hostel
HOSTEL

15 ⭐ MAP P126, B2

This quirky joint in a former fish factory combines austere four-, six- and eight-bed dorms with a cool theatre and live-music venue. In summer there's an active programme of plays, storytelling and music. Check online for the schedule. It also lets two apartments in Hellissandur. (☏ 833 8200; www.thefreezerhostel.com; Hafnargata 16, Rif; 🛜)

# Shopping
## Leir 7
ARTS & CRAFTS

16 🛍 MAP P126, A2

Artist Sigríður Erla produces beautiful ceramics from the fjord's dark clay at this pottery studio in the heart of Stykkishólmur. There's also woodcraft by Lára Gunnarsdóttir (www.smavinir.is). (☏ 894 0425; www.leir7.is; Aðalgata 20, Stykkishólmur; ⏲2-5pm Mon-Fri, to 4pm Sat)

## Gallerí Lundi
ARTS & CRAFTS

17 🛍 MAP P126, A1

Local handicrafts sold by friendly villagers. Also offers coffee. (☏ 893 5588; Aðalgata 4a, Stykkishólmur; ⏲12.30-6pm May-Sep)

# Explore ◈

# Borgarnes & Around

*For such a tiny place, Borgarnes bubbles with local life. One of the original settlement areas for the first Icelanders, it's loaded with history, and sits on a scenic promontory along the broad waters of Borgarfjörður. Inland, up the river-twined valley, lie heritage-rich farms, stone-strewn lava tubes and the highlands – the gateway to the ice caps beyond.*

*Spend your morning in Borgarnes learning about Iceland's Viking settlers and wild Egil's Saga at the Settlement Centre (p134), and touring the local saga sites such as Egil's farm. Lunch at the Settlement Centre's excellent on-site restaurant (p139) or stroll to waterfront cafe Englendingavík (p140) for casual eats and great views. Next, head inland to take a tour on enormous Langjökull (p137), or explore Iceland's largest lava tube Viðgelmir (p137). By now you'll be hungry. Head straight to smart Hótel Húsafell (p140), then soak at the fabulous Krauma spa (p137) – in summer it's open until 11pm.*

## Getting There & Around

🚗 Having your own vehicle gives you freedom.

🚌 Borgarnes is the major transfer point between Reykjavík and Snæfellsnes. Strætó bus 57 links Borgarnes with Reykjavík, while Strætó bus 58 goes to Stykkishólmur. Change to bus 82 for buses to Hellissandur and, from early May to mid-September, to Arnarstapi. Note that all services are reduced in winter.

## Borgarnes & Around Map on p136

## Top Sights 📷

# Witness the Story of Iceland at the Settlement Centre

*Borgarnes and its broad Borgarfjörður were the landing zone for several famous Icelandic settlers. Housed in a restored warehouse by the harbour, the fascinating Settlement Centre offers insights into the history of the settlers, and brings alive the story of one of the most famous – poet-warrior Egil Skallagrímsson (the man behind Egil's Saga), his amazing adventures and his equally intense family.*

📍 **MAP P136, B4**

Landnámssetur Íslands

📞 437 1600

www.settlementcentre.is

Brákarbraut 13-15

adult/child 2500kr/free

🕐 10am-9pm

## Settlement Exhibition

The Settlement Exhibition vividly covers the discovery and settlement of Iceland and gives a firm historical context in which to place your Icelandic visit. The interactive map illustrating where the first settlers made inroads is particularly fun, and the audio guide's recounting of settlers' stories illustrates how harsh it all was.

## Egil's Saga Exhibition

*Egil's Saga* is one of the most nuanced and action-packed of the sagas, and the exhibition uses creative art and diorama displays to recount how poet-warrior Egil Skallagrímsson's family settled the Borgarnes area, and how Egil became both a fierce and sensitive man, from his near murder by his father, to the death of his own sons.

## Local Landmarks

To explore how *Egil's Saga* ties to the Borgarnes area, download the Locatify SmartGuide smartphone or iPad app and load the 'Borg on the Moors' tour. It tells stories of local landmarks, which the Settlement Centre has marked with cairns, including **Brákin**, Egil's farm Borg á Mýrum, and **Skallagrímsgarður**, the burial mound of Egil's father and son.

## Egil's Farm

**Borg á Mýrum** (Rock in the Marshes; Rte 54; admission free), just northwest of Borgarnes, is where Skallagrímur Kveldúlfsson, Egil's father, made his farm at settlement. It was named for the large **rock** (borg) behind the farmstead. You can walk up to the **cairn** for super views. The small **cemetery** includes an ancient rune-inscribed gravestone. Ásmundur Sveinsson's **sculpture** represents Egil mourning the death of his sons and his rejuvenation in poetry.

★ **Top Tips**

o The museum is divided into two exhibitions; each takes about 30 minutes to visit. The cost for one exhibition is 1900kr and for two 2500kr.

o Kids under 14 are free.

o Detailed multi-lingual audio guides are included.

o Leave time to explore area sites from *Egil's Saga*.

o In summer, reserve ahead for dinner at the Settlement Centre restaurant.

✗ **Take a Break**

The Settlement Centre has a top-notch restaurant (p139) built into the rock face that serves modern Icelandic fare.

If you feel like strolling the town, fun Englendingavík (p140) offers a more casual cafe vibe with great water views.

**Borgarnes & Around**

0 ——— 10 miles
0 ——— 20 km

Hvammsfjörður

Hlíðarvatn

Hítarvatn

Langavatn

BORGARBYGGÐ

Arnarvatnsheiði

Tvídægra

Haukadalur

Haukadalsá

Stóra-Vatnshorn

Erpsstaðir

Baula (934m)

Hraunsnef

Grábrók

Bifröst

Munaðarnes

Svignaskarð

Deildartunguhver

Hreðavatn

Kleppjárnsreykir

Krauma

Reykholt

Icelandic Goat Centre

Kaldá

Barnafoss

Hraunfossar

Húsafell

Into the Glacier

Víðgelmir – the Cave

Hallmundarhraun

Eiríksjökull (1675m)

Langjökull

Hafafell (1167m)

Geitlandsjökull (1390m)

Þórisjökull (1350m)

Kaldidalur Corridor

Ok (1190m)

Flókadalur

Borgarfjörður

Hvanneyri

Hafnarfjall

Skorradalsvatn

Borgarnes

Settlement Centre

# Sights

## Langjökull
GLACIER

1 MAP P136, F3

The Langjökull ice cap is the second largest glacier in Iceland, and the closest major glacier to Reykjavík. It's accessed from the 4WD Kaldidalur or Kjölur tracks, and its closest access village in West Iceland is Húsafell. Do not attempt to drive up onto the glacier yourself. Tours depart from Reykjavík or Húsafell: the Into the Glacier ice cave is a major tourist attraction, **Mountaineers of Iceland** (580 9900; www.mountaineers.is) offers snowmobiling, and **Dog Sledding** (863 6733; www.dogsledding.is; tours from 19,900kr) sometimes has summertime dog-sledding tours.

## Into the Glacier
CAVE

2 MAP P136, E3

This enormous (300m-long) human-made tunnel and series of caves head into Langjökull glacier at 1260m above sea level. The glistening, LED-lit tunnel and caves opened in 2015 and contain exhibitions, a cafe and even a small chapel for those who want to tie the knot inside a glacier. Tours leave from Húsafell (shuttle adult/child 2000kr/free) or the glacier edge (tour adult/child 19,500kr/free) in summer if you have a 4WD. Tours also leave from Reykjavík (29,900kr), and there are many combo tours (eg snowmobiling, helicopter). (Langjökull Ice Cave; 578 2550; www.intotheglacier.is)

## Viðgelmir – the Cave
CAVE

3 MAP P136, E3

The easiest lava tube to visit, and the largest in Iceland, 1100-year-old, 1.5km-long Viðgelmir is located on private property near the farmstead Fljótstunga. It sparkles with ever-changing rock formations and has a stable walkway within it on which tours are conducted; helmet and torch included. (783 3600; www.thecave.is; off Rte 518; tour adult/child from 6500kr/free)

## Deildartunguhver
HOT SPRING

4 MAP P136, C3

Find Europe's biggest hot spring, Deildartunguhver, about 5km west of Reykholt, just off Rte 50, near the junction with Rte 518. Look for billowing clouds of steam, which rise from scalding water bubbling from the ground (180L per second and 100°C). There's a new bathing complex, Krauma, and also a restaurant.

## Krauma
GEOTHERMAL BATHS

5 MAP P136, C3

Water from neighbouring Deildartunguhver heats this modern outdoor bathing complex with five multi-temperature hot-pots and two steam baths. Guests also enjoy a relaxation room and the brave can get their circulation going with a cold tub dip. Attached is a bistro with Icelandic cuisine (mains 2700kr to 3800kr). (555 6066; www.krauma. is; Deildartunguhver, Rte 50; adult/child 3800kr/free; 11am-11pm mid-Jun–mid-Aug, to 9pm rest of year)

# Seeing the Northern Lights

Topping countless bucket lists and filling Instagram feeds, the Northern Lights (aurora borealis) are a magnet drawing cool-weather visitors, who arrive with fingers crossed and necks craned skywards.

## What Are They?

The souls of the dead according to the Inuit; the spirits of unmarried women according to Scandinavian folklore. Modern science, though, has a different take.

The magical curtains of colour are the result of solar wind – a stream of particles from the sun that collides with oxygen, nitrogen and hydrogen in the upper atmosphere. These collisions produce the haunting greens and magentas as the earth's magnetic field draws the wind towards the polar regions.

## Where & How Can I See Them?

Many tour companies offer 'Northern Lights tours' (by boat, jeep or bus) – they are essentially taking you to an area with less light pollution to increase viewing odds. You can do this yourself, too, though inexperienced winter drivers should not chase clear skies in remote, snowy areas.

Head to recommended viewing spots on the outskirts of Reykjavík (these include Grótta lighthouse at Seltjarnarnes, or Öskjuhlíð hill), or book a few nights at a rural inn.

Viewings can begin as early as late August. Mid-September to mid-April is the 'official' season. On average, auroras are wice as common near equinox (around September/October and March/April).

## Predicting Activity

Predicting the likelihood of a display is close to impossible, but various apps and alerts can help. Try the comprehensive website of the Icelandic Met Office (http://en.vedur.is/weather/forecasts/aurora) or www.easyaurora.com.

---

## Hraunfossar
WATERFALL

6 ◉ MAP P136, D3

The name of this spectacular waterfall translates to 'Lava Field Waterfall' because the crystalline water streams out from below the lava field all around. Walk a little further on the marked trail to reach Barnafoss, another churning chute. Find the turn-off on the north side of Rte 518, 6.5km west of Húsafell.

### Icelandic Goat Centre FARM

7 ⊙ MAP P136, D3

Farm workers walk you through pretty fields with endangered Icelandic goats. The farm's most famous resident is Casanova, a bright-eyed goat who had a starring turn in *Game of Thrones* (running from a dragon). Find the farm on dirt-road Rte 523, northeast of Reykholt. Coffee or tea included. (☏ 435 1448; www. geitur.is; Rte 523, Háafell; tour adult/child 1500/750kr; ⊙1-6pm Jun-Aug)

### Hafnarfjall HIKING

8 ⊙ MAP P136, B4

The dramatically sheer mountain Hafnarfjall (844m) rises south across the fjord from Borgarnes. You can climb it (7km) from the trailhead on Rte 1, near the southern base of the causeway into Borgarnes. Be careful of slippery scree cliffs once you ascend. You'll get sweeping views from the top.

## Eating

### Settlement Centre Restaurant INTERNATIONAL €€

9 ⊗ MAP P136, B4

The Settlement Centre's restaurant, set in a light-filled room built into the rock face, is airy, upbeat and one of the region's best bets for food. Choose from traditional Icelandic and international eats (lamb, fish stew etc). The lunch buffet (11.30am to 3pm) is very popular. Book ahead for dinner. (☏ 437 1600; www. landnam.is; Brákarbraut 13, Borgarnes; lunch buffet 2200kr, mains 2200-4600kr; ⊙10am-9pm; 🛜)

Hraunfossar

KONDRATEV ALEXEY/SHUTTERSTOCK ©

## Hótel Húsafell ICELANDIC €€€

The outstanding restaurant in this chic hotel near Langjökull (see 2  Map p136, F3) serves creative Icelandic cuisine showcasing superb ingredients and refined presentation. Art is the original work of local artist Páll Guðmundsson, and spectacular views are the work of Iceland. (☏ 435 1551; www.hotelhusafell.com; Rte 518; mains lunch 2600-5400kr, dinner 4800-7600kr; P)

## Englendingavík CAFE €€

Casual and friendly, with a wonderful waterfront deck, Englendingavík serves good homemade dishes, from cakes to full meals of roast lamb or fresh fish. It has an attached guesthouse (doubles with shared bathroom from 27,400kr) in a restored building with good bay views. Near the Settlement Centre Restaurant (see 9 Map p136, B4). (☏ 555 1400; www.englendingavik.is; Skúlagata 17, Borgarnes; mains 2500-5100kr; ⏱ 11.30am-11pm May-Sep, reduced hours Apr & Oct; 🛜 ✏)

## Skemma Cafe CAFE €

Tucked away in the village of Hvanneyri, 12km east of Borgarnes, in a renovated building that dates from 1896, this small cafe has a sunny deck and soups, waffles, cakes and coffee. It's located near Ullarselið (see 12 Map p136, B4) (Skemman Kaffihús; ☏ 868 8626; www.facebook.com/skemmancafe; Agricultural Museum of Iceland complex, Hvanneyri; snacks 900-1350kr; ⏱ noon-5pm Tue-Sun Jun–mid-Aug)

## Hraunfossar Cafe CAFE €€

This welcoming cafe just back from Hraunfossar (see 6 Map p136, D3) has wide decks and a solid menu of basic soup, burgers, salads and snacks. (☏ 435 1155; www.hraunfossar.is; Rte 518; mains 1900-2700kr; ⏱ 10am-8pm Jun-Aug, reduced hours rest of year)

---

## Farm Food  🍽

Like to eat your way across the countryside? Make a beeline to **Erpsstaðir** (Map p136, C1; ☏ 868 0357; www.erpsstadir.is; Rte 60; cowshed tour adult/child 600kr/free; ⏱ 11am-6pm mid-Jun–mid-Aug, 1-5pm mid-May–mid-Jun & mid-Aug–mid-Sep; 🐾). Like a mirage for sweet-toothed wanderers, this dairy farm amid the waterfalls of Rte 60 (between Búðardalur and the Ring Road) specialises in delicious homemade ice cream (400kr). Want more guidance? Join a **Crisscross Food Tour** (☏ 897 6140; www.crisscross.is) across West Iceland, with farm stops, snacks and a meal (full day 39,500kr) while taking in waterfalls and lava fields.

OSCAR BJARNASON/GETTY ©

Hafnarfjall (p139)

# Drinking

## Steðji Brugghús BREWERY

10 MAP P136, C4

This little family-run brewhouse 25km northeast of Borgarnes off Rte 50 has a good range of local beers, from strawberry beer to lager and seasonal beers. Try them all in the microbrewery's tasting room. (📞896 5001; www.stedji.com; tasting 1500kr; ⏰1-5pm Mon-Sat)

# Shopping

## Ljómalind MARKET

11 MAP P136, B4

A long-standing collaboration between local producers, this packed farmers market sits at the edge of Borgarnes near the roundabout. It stocks everything from fresh dairy products from Erpsstaðir and organic meat to locally made bath products, handmade wool sweaters, jewellery and all manner of imaginative collectables. (📞437 1400; www.ljomalind.is; Brúartorg 4, Borgarnes; ⏰10am-6pm May-Sep, noon-5pm Oct-Apr)

## Ullarselið CLOTHING, ARTS & CRAFTS

12 MAP P136, B4

Find your way to the village of Hvanneyri, and in among fjordside homes you'll find this fantastic wool centre. Handmade sweaters, scarves, hats and blankets share space with skeins of hand-spun yarn, and interesting bone and shell buttons. Plus there are needles and patterns to get you started. (📞437 0077; www.ull.is; Hvanneyri; ⏰11am-5pm Jun-Aug, 1-5pm Thu-Sat Sep-May)

# Survival Guide

# Before You Go

## Book Your Stay

○ June through August accommodation books out entirely; reservations are essential.

○ Reykjavík 101 is the central district, best for easy walking around town.

○ Reykjavík has loads of accommodation choices, with hostels, midrange guesthouses (often with shared bathrooms, kitchen and lounge) and business-class hotels galore.

○ Prices are high. Plan for hostels, camping or short-term apartment rentals to save money.

○ Most places open year-round and many offer discounts or variable pricing online.

## Best Budget

**Reykjavík Downtown Hostel** (www.hostel.is) Top dorm digs or private rooms in this HI hostel offer some of the best bargains in the city centre.

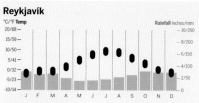

**Reykjavík**

°C/°F Temp — Rainfall inches/mm

## When to Go

**High Season (Jun–Aug)** Big crowds. Prices peak; accommodation bookings are essential. Endless daylight and plentiful festivals.

**Shoulder (May & Sep)** Breezy weather, occasional snows.

Smaller crowds and lower prices.

**Low Season (Oct–Apr)** Long nights usher in the Northern Lights. Activities include skiing, snowshoeing and visiting ice caves.

**KEX Hostel** (ww.kex hostel.is) A favourite for its off-beat decor and good bar.

**101 Hostel** (101hostel@mail.com) Friendly, homey, history-rich hostel in an enviably central location.

**Loki 101** (www.loki101.is) Simple, central B&B near Hallgrímskirkja.

## Best Midrange

**Forsæla Apartment-house** (www.apartment house.is) Cosy B&B rooms or apartments get top marks for comfort.

**Nest Apartments** (www.nestapartments.is) Small, comfortable, well-appointed flats with a great location.

**Galtafell Guesthouse** (www.galtafell.com) Comfortable doubles and apartments fill a restored, beautiful mansion.

**Loft Hostel** (www.lofthostel.is) Smart, central and with great nightlife, this is one of the town's best hostels.

## Best Top End

**Consulate Hotel Reykjavík** (www.curio collection3.hilton.com)

History-rich hotel where the service is just so.

**Kvosin Downtown** (www.kvosinhotel.is) Some of these sleek apartments in the heart of Old Reykjavík offer super views.

**Reykjavík Residence** (www.rrhotel.is) Rooms and apartments in beautifully reno-vated mansions near Laugavegur.

**Alda Hotel** (www.aldahotel.is) A boutique beauty amid shopping central Laugavegur.

# Arriving in Reykjavík & Southwest Iceland

## Keflavík International Airport

Iceland's primary international **airport** (KEF; ☏ 425 6000; www.kef airport.is; Reykjanesbraut; ⊙24hr) is 48km west of Reykjavík. **Flybus** (☏ 580 5400; www.re.is; 1-way ticket 2950kr; 🛜), **Airport Express** (☏ 540

1313; www.airportexpress.is; 🛜) and **Airport Direct** (☏ 497 5000; www.reyk javiksightseeing.is/airport -direct; 1-way/return ticket from 5500/10,000kr; 🛜) provide excellent bus links to the city.

**Strætó** (☏ 540 2700; www.straeto.is) bus 55 also connects the city's BSÍ Bus Terminal and the airport (1840kr, nine daily Monday to Friday in summer). Cars can be rented from the airport – pre-booking is highly recommended.

Getting a taxi into the city is relatively expensive (16,100kr).

## Reykjavík Domestic Airport

o In central Reykjavík, just 2km south of

Tjörnin. Sightseeing services, domestic flights and those to/ from Greenland and the Faroe Islands fly here.

o There's a taxi rank at the airport.

o Bus 15 stops near the Air Iceland Connect terminal and goes on to the Hlemmur bus stop.

# Getting Around

## Air

**Air Iceland Connect** (☏ 570 3030; www. airicelandconnect.is; Rey-kjavík Domestic Airport) Main domestic airline, operates flights and sightseeing services.

---

### Useful Accommodation Websites

**Airbnb** (www.airbnb.com) Private rooms, apartments and houses.

**Booking.com** Popular and thorough, espe-cially in the countryside.

**CouchSurfing** (www.couchsurfing.com) Network of travellers hosting travellers.

**Hey Iceland** (www.heyiceland.is) Experi-enced Icelandic travel agency.

**Lonely Planet** (lonelyplanet.com/iceland/ hotels) Recommendations and bookings.

## Car

o Totally unnecessary in central Reykjavík.

o Hiring wheels makes exploring the rest of Iceland easier.

o Car and camper hire for the countryside are available at both airports, the BSÍ Bus Terminal and some city locations.

o City speed limits are usually 50km/h (30mph) unless posted otherwise.

o Seatbelts are required.

o It is illegal to use a mobile phone while driving.

## Local Bus

o **Strætó** ( 540 2700; www.straeto.is) operates regional buses and regular buses around Reykjavík and its suburbs (Seltjarnarnes, Kópavogur, Garðabær, Hafnarfjörður and Mosfellsbær).

o Single fares are 460kr; buy tickets at the bus terminal, pay on board (no change given) or by using the Strætó app.

o The Reykjavík City Card also acts as a Strætó bus pass.

o Many free maps like *Welcome to Reykjavík City Map* also include bus-route maps.

o Buses run from 7am until 11pm or midnight daily (from 11am on Sunday). Services depart at 15-minute or 30-minute intervals.

o A limited night-bus service runs until 4.30am on Friday and Saturday.

## Regional Bus & Tours

o Bus services are ever-changing; get up-to-date information on schedules and fares from bus company websites and tourist offices.

o The free Public Transport in Iceland (www.publictransport.is) map has a good overview of routes.

o You can travel from Reykjavík by day tour (most offer hotel pickup), or use Strætó or one of the other companies, getting on and off their scheduled buses. There are a multitude of bus transport passes.

o The bus network operates frequently from around mid-May to mid-September. Outside these months services to remoter regions can be less frequent (or nonexistent).

Strætó operates Reykjavík long-distance buses from **Mjódd Bus Terminal** ( 540 2700; www.bus.is; ⊙ticket office 7am-6pm Mon-Fri, 10am-6pm Sat, 12.30-6pm Sun), 8km southeast of the city centre, which is served by local buses 3, 4, 11, 12, 17, 21 and 24. For long-distance buses only you can use cash, credit/debit card with PIN or (wads of) bus tickets.

**Reykjavík Excursions** (Kynnisferðir; 580 5400; www.re.is), as well as its Flybus, uses the **BSÍ Bus Terminal** ( 580 5400; www.bsi.is; Vatnsmýrarvegur 10; 🕿) – pronounced 'bee-ess-ee' – located around 2km south of the city centre. There's a ticketing desk, tourist brochures, lockers, luggage storage (www.luggagelockers.is), Budget car hire and a cafeteria with wi-fi.

The terminal is served by Reykjavík buses 1, 3, 5, 6, 14 and 15. Reykjavík Excursions offers pre-booked hotel pick-up to bring you to the terminal. Some **Grayline** (Iceland Excursions; ☏ 540 1313; www.grayline.is; Hafnarstræti 20) buses also stop there.

**Sterna** (☏ 551 1166; www.icelandbybus.is; 🛜) has sales and departures from the Harpa concert hall. Buses travel around the southern Ring Road and to tourist highlights.

**Trex** (☏ 587 6000; www.trex.is) departs from the Main Tourist Office (p150), Kringlan's Shell petrol station or Reykjavík Campsite. Buses go to Þórsmörk and Landmannalaugar in the south.

# Essential Information

## Accessible Travel

Iceland, especially when you leave Reykjavík, can be trickier than many places in northern Europe when it comes to access for travellers with disabilities.

### Dos & Don'ts

○ Strip naked and shower thoroughly before entering a hot-pot or pool. Failure to do this will cause offence.

○ Remove your shoes when entering someone's home.

○ Smoking is banned in public places, bars and restaurants.

○ It's not customary to tip taxis or in restaurants.

For information, contact the National Association of People with Disabilities, **Þekkingarmiðstöð Sjálfsbjargar** (Sjálfsbjörg Knowledge Centre; ☏ 550 0118; www.thekkingar midstod.is; Hátún 12, Reykjavík).

God Adgang (www.godadgang.dk) can find accessible service providers.

For tailor-made accessible trips, try Iceland Unlimited (www.icelandunlimited.is). Grayline and Reykjavík Excursions have some accessible options.

Reykjavík's city buses have a 'kneeling' function to improve accessibility. Elsewhere, public buses are unlikely to have ramps or lifts.

## Business Hours

Opening hours vary throughout the year (even in Reykjavík some places are closed outside the high season).

Hours tend to be far longer from June to August, and shorter from September to May. Standard opening hours:

**Banks** 9am to 4pm Monday to Friday. Arion banki at Kringlan opens later and on Saturday (10am to 6pm) and Sunday (1pm to 6pm).

**Cafe-bars** 11am to 1am Sunday to Thursday, 10am to between 3am and 6am Friday to Saturday

**Cafes** 10am to 6pm

**Offices** 9am to 5pm Monday to Friday

**Petrol stations** 8am to 10pm or 11pm; many have 24-hour pay-at-the-pump machines that require PIN numbers for credit/debit cards

**Post offices** 9am to 6pm Monday to Friday (to 4pm in the countryside)

**Restaurants** 11.30am to 2.30pm and 6pm to 9pm or 10pm; later if they're also bars

**Shops** 10am to 6pm Monday to Friday, 10am to 4pm Saturday; some open Sunday in Reykjavík malls and major shopping strips

**Supermarkets** 9am to 10pm (closing earlier in the countryside); 10-11 supermarkets often open 24 hours, while Bónus has unusual hours

**Vínbúðin** Opening hours for these government-run alcohol stores are variable; many outside Reykjavík only open for a couple of hours per day

## Discount Cards

**Reykjavík City Card** (www.citycard.is; 24/48/72hr 3800/5400/6500kr) offers admission to 10 of Reykjavík's municipal swimming/thermal pools and most of the main galleries and museums, plus discounts on some tours, shops and entertainment. It also gives free travel on the city's Strætó buses and on the ferry to Viðey.

The 24-hour **Children's City Card** (1600kr) is less useful, since kids enter free at many museums anyway. Both cards are available at the Main Tourist Office (p150), some travel agencies, 10-11 supermarkets, HI hostels and some hotels.

## Electricity

Type C
220V/50Hz

Type F
230V/50Hz

## Emergency & Important Numbers

To call from outside Iceland, dial your international access code, Iceland's country code, and then the seven-digit number. There are no area codes in Iceland.

**Emergency services** (☎112)

**Directory enquiries** (☎118)

**Iceland country code – dialling in** (☎354)

**International access code – dialling out** (☎00)

**Weather** (☎ 902, press 1 after the introduction)

**Road condition information** (☎ 1777)

## Money

o The Icelandic unit of currency is the króna (plural krónur), written as kr here, often written elsewhere as ISK.

o Credit cards are used everywhere; ATMs are throughout the centre.

o While credit cards are ubiquitous, many transactions (such as petrol purchases) require a PIN. Make sure you have one before you leave home.

o Tipping is not required, as service and VAT (value added tax) are included.

## Public Holidays

**New Year's Day** 1 January

**Easter** March or April; Maundy Thursday and Good Friday to Easter Monday (changes annually)

**First Day of Summer** First Thursday after 18 April

**Labour Day** 1 May

**Ascension Day** May or June (changes

## Money-Saving Tips

o Anyone who has a permanent address outside Iceland can claim a tax refund on purchases when they spend over 6000kr (at a single point of sale). Look for stores with a 'tax-free shopping' sign in the window, and ask for a form.

o Buy alcohol when you arrive at Keflavík International Airport Duty Free for the steepest discounts.

o The best bar prices are at happy hours. Download the smartphone app Reykjavík Appy Hour.

annually)

**Whit Sunday and Whit Monday** May or June (changes annually)

**National Day** 17 June

**Commerce Day** First Monday in August

**Christmas** 24 to 26 December

**New Year's Eve** 31 December

## Safe Travel

Iceland has a very low crime rate. In general any risks you'll face while travelling are related to road safety, unpredictable weather and unique geological conditions.

**Safetravel** (www. safetravel.is) Initiative of the Icelandic As-

sociation for Search and Rescue (ICE-SAR). It helps minimise your risks.

**112 Iceland** App for smartphones (useful in emergencies); explains procedures for leaving a travel plan with ICE-SAR or a friend/contact.

## Telephone Services

o Online phone book: http://en.ja.is (people are listed by their first names).

o Buy prepaid SIM cards and top-up credit at bookstores, grocery stores, petrol stations and on Icelandair flights.

o Iceland Telecom Síminn (www.siminn. is/prepaid) has the

greatest network coverage and Vodafone (www.vodafone.is/en/prepaid) isn't far behind.

‣ Both companies have voice-and-data starter packs including local SIM cards; Síminn's costs 2900kr and includes either 10GB data, or 5GB and 50 minutes of international talk time.

‣ EU citizens don't face roaming surcharges in Iceland. If you're not from the EU (or EAA), you can get cheaper calls by buying an Icelandic SIM card and putting it in your own (unlocked) phone.

## Toilets

Your best bet is to find toilets in hotels, cafes and restaurants.

## Tourist Information

### Main Tourist Office

(Upplýsingamiðstöð Ferðamanna; Map p40, C3; ☎ 411 6040; www.visitreykjavik.is; Ráðhús, Tjarnargata 11; ☺ 8am-8pm; ☎) Friendly staff and mountains of free brochures, plus maps, Reykjavík City Card and Strætó city bus tickets. Books accommodation, tours and activities.

### Inspired By Iceland

(www.inspiredbyiceland.com) Iceland-wide information.

## Visas

‣ Iceland is one of 26 European Schengen Convention countries.

‣ For EU and Schengen countries, no visa is required for stays of up to three months.

‣ For citizens of Australia, Canada, Japan, New Zealand and the USA, no visa is required for tourist visits of up to three months. Total stay within the Schengen area must not exceed three months in any six-month period. For citizens of other countries, check online at www.utl.is.

# Language

Most Icelanders speak English, however, any attempts to speak the local language will be much appreciated. If you read our pronunciation guides as if they were English, you'll be understood.

## Basics

**Hello.**
*Halló.* ha·loh

**Good morning.**
*Góðan daginn.* gohth-ahn dai-in

**Goodbye.**
*Bless.* bles

**Thank you**
*Takk./ Takk fyrir.* tak/ tak fi·rir

**Excuse me.**
*Afsakið.* af·sa·kidh

**Sorry.**
*Fyrirgefðu.* fi·rir·gev·dhu

**Yes.**
*Já.* yow

**No.**
*Nei.* nay

**How are you?**
*Hvað segir* kvadh se·yir
*þú gott?* thoo got

**Fine. And you?**
*Allt fínt. En þú?* alt feent en thoo

**What's your name?**
*Hvað heitir þú?* kvadh hay·tir thoo

**My name is ...**
*Ég heiti ...* yekh hay·ti ...

**Do you speak English?**
*Talar þú ensku?* ta·lar thoo ens·ku

**I don't understand.**
*Ég skil ekki.* yekh skil e·ki

## Eating & Drinking

**What would you recommend?**
*Hverju mælir þú með?*
kver·yu mai·lir thoo medh

**Do you have vegetarian food?**
*Hafið þið grænmetisrétti?*
ha·vidh thidh grain·me·tis·rye·ti

**I'll have a ...**
*Ég ætla að fá ...* yekh ait·la adh fow ...

**Cheers!**
*Skál!* skowl

**I'd like a/the ..., please.**
*Get ég fengið ..., takk.*
get yekh fen·gidh ..., tak

**table for**
*borð fyrir* bordh fi·rir

**bill**
*reikninginn* rayk·nin·gin

**drink list**
*vínseðillinn* veen·se·dhit·lin

**menu**
*matseðillinn* mat·se·dhit·lin

**that dish**
*þennan rétt* the·nan ryet

## Shopping

**I'm looking for ...**
*Ég leita að ...* yekh lay·ta adh ...

**How much is it?**
*Hvað kostar þetta?* kvadh kos·tar the·ta

**That's too expensive.**
*Þetta er of dýrt.* the·ta er of deert

## Emergencies

**Help!**
*Hjálp!*     hyowlp

**Go away!**
*Farðu!*     far·dhu

**Call ...!**
*Hringdu á ...!*     hring·du ow ...!

  **a doctor**
  *lækni*     laik·ni

  **the police**
  *lögregluna*     leu·rekh·lu·na

**I'm lost.**
*Ég er villtur/villt.* (m/f)
yekh er vil·tur/vilt

**Where are the toilets?**
*Hvar er snyrtingin?*   kvar er snir·tin·gin

## Numbers

| | | |
|---|---|---|
| 1 | *einn* | aydn |
| 2 | *tveir* | tvayr |
| 3 | *þrír* | threer |
| 4 | *fjórir* | fyoh·rir |
| 5 | *fimm* | fim |
| 6 | *sex* | seks |
| 7 | *sjö* | syeu |
| 8 | *átta* | ow·ta |
| 9 | *níu* | nee·u |
| 10 | *tíu* | tee·u |
| 20 | *tuttugu* | tu·tu·gu |
| 30 | *þrjátíu* | throw·tee·u |
| 40 | *fjörutíu* | fyeur·tee·u |
| 50 | *fimmtíu* | fim·tee·u |
| 100 | *hundrað* | hun·dradh |

## Directions

**Where's the (hotel)?**
*Hvar er (hótelið)?*   kvar er
                         (hoh·te·lidh)

**Can you show me (on the map)?**
*Geturðu sýnt mér (á kortinu)?*
ge·tur·dhu seent myer (ow *kor*·ti·nu)

**What's your address?**
*Hvert er heimilisfangið þitt?*
kvert er *hay*·mi·lis·fan·gidh thit

## Transport

**Is this the ...**
*Er þetta ...*     er the·ta ...
**to (Akureyri)?**
*til (Akureyrar)?*     til (a·ku·ray·rar)

**boat**
*ferjan*     fer·yan

**bus**
*rútan*     roo·tan

**plane**
*flugvélin*     flukh·vye·lin

**What time's**
*Hvenær fer ...*     kve·nair fer ...
**the ... bus?**
*strætisvagninn?*     strai·tis·vag·nin

**One ... ticket (to Reykjavík), please.**
*Einn miða ... (til Reykjavíkur), tak.*
aitn mi·dha ... (til rayk·ya·vee·kur) takk.

**How much is it to ...?**
*Hvað kostar til ... ?*   kvadh kos·tar til ...

**Please stop here.**
*Stoppaðu hér, takk.*
sto·pa·dhu hyer tak

**Please take me to (this address).**
*Viltu aka mér til (þessa staðar).*
vil·tu a·ka myer til (the·sa sta·dhar).

# Behind the Scenes

## Send Us Your Feedback

We love to hear from travellers – your comments help make our books better. We read every word, and we guarantee that your feedback goes straight to the authors. Visit **lonelyplanet.com/contact** to submit your updates and suggestions.

Note: We may edit, reproduce and incorporate your comments in Lonely Planet products such as guidebooks, websites and digital products, so let us know if you don't want your comments reproduced or your name acknowledged. For a copy of our privacy policy visit lonelyplanet.com/privacy.

## Belinda's Thanks

What an extraordinary opportunity – to drive pitted roads beside vast fjords, soaking in hot-pots along the way. Thanks as big as those mountains go to the whole Lonely Planet team and all who've shared information and inspiration, including Magnus in Djúpavík, Charis in Reykjanes, Kári and Thomas in Ísafjörður and Eyþor in Flateyri. And to the warmest, wisest collaborators a writer could wish for: Alexis Averbuck and Carolyn Bain – raising a *snúður* to you both!

## Alexis' Thanks

Life in Iceland wouldn't be the same without the brilliant support of Carolyn Bain. She shared her friends and her ace tips on this great land with utmost generosity.

## This Book

This 4th edition of Lonely Planet's *Reykjavík & Southwest Iceland* guidebook was curated by Belinda Dixon and researched and written by Belinda Dixon, Alexis Averbuck, Carolyn Bain and Jade Bremner.

This guidebook was produced by the following:

**Destination Editor**
Clifton Wilkinson

**Senior Product Editor**
Dan Bolger, Genna Patterson

**Regional Senior Cartographer**
Valentina Kremenchutskaya, Julie Sheridan

**Product Editors**
Carolyn Boicos, Katie Connolly, Claire Rourke

**Book Designer**
Fergal Condon

**Assisting Editors**
Judith Bamber, Gabrielle Innes, Kate Morgan, Monique Perrin, Rachel Rawling

**Cover Researcher**
Meri Blazevski

**Thanks to**
Alex Conroy, Catherine Naghten, Martine Power, Jocelyne Rigal, Claire Storey, Jeanne Stuart

Folks such as Halldór at Visit North Iceland and Addi, Anton, Stefán, Jóhanna, Finnur, Villi, Elisabet and Odinn and others I met along the way graciously shared their stories and their ideas. Thanks, too, to my own personal peachy King of the Mountains, RVB.

## Carolyn's Thanks

Heartfelt thanks go to Icelandic friends, old and new, for making my relocation to Reykjavík such a rewarding move. As ever, a huge cast of locals, travellers and expats helped make this research project a delight, and I'm grateful to all of them for helping me see more, understand more and enjoy more. Cheers to Clifton Wilkinson for the job, and bouquets to my co-authors for their collaborative spirit, especially to Alexis and Belinda for sparking gin-soaked dreams of future projects.

## Jade's Thanks

Thanks to Destination Editor Clifton Wilkinson for his superb destination and publishing knowledge. Plus, everyone working behind the scenes on this project – Cheree Broughton, Dianne, Jane, Neill Coen, Evan Godt and Helen Elfer. Last but not least, thanks to my travelling accomplice Harriet Sinclair, who joined me for a few epic days scaling Hekla volcano and walking the legendary Fimmvörðuháls trail.

## Acknowledgements

Cover photograph: Blue Lagoon, Steve Allen/Getty ©

Photographs p30: (top) Bahadir Yeniceri/Shutterstock ©; (bottom) Dennis van de Water/Shutterstock ©

Photographs p90: (top) Dave Porter/Getty Images ©; (bottom) Brian Maudsley/Shutterstock ©

# Index

See also separate subindexes for:

⊗ Eating p158
🍷 Drinking p158
🎭 Entertainment p159
🛍 Shopping p159

Sights 000
Map Pages **000**

# Our Writers

### Belinda Dixon

Only happy when her feet are suitably sandy, Belinda has been (gleefully) travelling, researching and writing for Lonely Planet since 2006. It has seen her soaking in hot-pots in Iceland's Westfjords, marvelling at Stonehenge at sunrise and gazing at Verona's frescoes.

### Alexis Averbuck

Alexis has travelled and lived all over the world, from Sri Lanka to Ecuador, Zanzibar and Antarctica. In recent years she's been living on the Greek island of Hydra and exploring her adopted homeland; sampling oysters in Brittany; and adventuring along Iceland's surreal lava fields, sparkling fjords and glacier tongues.

### Carolyn Bain

A travel writer and editor for more than 20 years, Carolyn has lived, worked and studied in various corners of the globe. She has authored more than 50 Lonely Planet titles, with her all-time favourite research destination being Iceland.

### Jade Bremner

Jade has been a journalist for more than a decade. She has lived in and reported on four different regions. Wherever she goes she finds action sports to try, the weirder the better, and it's no coincidence many of her favourite places have some of the best waves in the world.

**Published by Lonely Planet Global Limited**
CRN 554153
4th edition – Mar 2022
ISBN 978 1 787017 51 1
© Lonely Planet 2022   Photographs © as indicated 2022
10 9 8 7 6 5 4 3 2 1
Printed in Singapore